LIVIN' IN DRUM

'It is the kind of verse that come
keep his heart up. It rhymes and sings. It goes to the tunes
you pick up from a fiddler at fairs.'
Helen Waddell

'These verses are in the best sense true to the essential
spirit of the Ulster folk, a genuine literary expression of
their soul in its tenderness and its strength'
Northern Whig

'As different from the typical anaemic poetry of today as
rich cream is from watery tea'
Derry Journal

Livin' in Drumlister

The Collected Ballads and Verses
of

W.F. Marshall
`The Bard of Tyrone'

THE
BLACKSTAFF
PRESS

First published in 1983 by
The Blackstaff Press Limited
3 Galway Park, Dundonald, Belfast, BT16 0AN, Northern Ireland
with the assistance of
The Arts Council of Northern Ireland

Reprinted 1983 (twice), 1984 (with corrections), 1987, 1988

Printed in Northern Ireland by
The Universities Press Limited

British Library Cataloguing in Publication Data
Marshall, W.F.
    Livin' in Drumlister.
    I. Title
    821'.914   PR6025.A/
ISBN 0-85640-293-1

CONTENTS

Unpublished poems

FOREWORD

'The Bard of Tyrone', the Reverend William Forbes Marshall, BA, LLB, DD, MRIA, – Bill Marshall to his friends – was born in County Tyrone, in Drumragh, Omagh, on 8 May 1888. He was the second of the three sons of Charles Marshall, the principal of Sixmilecross National School, and of the former Miss Mary Forbes. Young W.F. went first to his father's school and then continued his education at the Royal School, Dungannon – 'The good old school'. His 'R.S.D.: a school ballad' has been adopted as the school song, and has been sung lustily on academic occasions by generations of Royal School boys. He attended Queen's College, Galway, an associate college of the Royal University of Ireland, from which he graduated in Arts in 1908.

His poetic muse was first revealed in his college days. Some extant poems of that period, ranging from philosophising on nature to a parody of Keats' 'Ode on a Grecian urn', show the scope of his latent talent.

In the autumn of 1908, he and his elder brother, R.L., began their theological course at The Presbyterian College, Belfast, familiarly known as Assembly's College. Their colleagues referred to W.F. as 'Wee' Marshall and his brother as 'Big' Marshall. R.L. Marshall was minister in Maghera Presbyterian Church, and later Professor of English and Lecturer in Catechetics at Magee University College, Londonderry. W.F., recalling some of the students' impish escapades, wrote, 'There were earnest youths in the class who disapproved of these activities, and declared them unethical which, to my mind, is not so good a term for them as childish. At the same time, for us to concern ourselves with notes would have been idiotic, seeing that Big Marshall was there to look after that end of it, and seemed to get some relish out of doing so.'

During his Theological Course he read Law in preparation for an extern degree, and graduated LLB from The Royal University of Ireland in 1910.

He was licensed as a probationer for the ministry of the Presbyterian Church by the Presbytery of Omagh in 1912, and became assistant to the Very Rev William M'Kean, DD, in First Ballymacarrett Presbyterian Church, Belfast. Dr M'Kean's son, John, who followed in his father's footsteps by entering the ministry and also becoming Moderator of the General Assembly, formed a lifelong friendship with W.F. during which many an hour was spent in a boat fishing Lough Melvin.

W.F. was ordained and installed in Aughnacloy on 26 June 1913 – 'a three-hour journey by pony and trap from Sixmilecross'.

A short time after his ordination he was invited to preach at an open-air service. The hymns were selected from an interdenominational hymn book. He announced the first hymn – 'Hymn number nine' – and was promptly interrupted by a puritan protestor who objected to 'them human hymns' (that is, non-biblical) being sung. The crowd waited, hushed, to see how 'the new broom' would react. 'I announced hymn number nine,' said W.F., 'and read the first line, "All people that on earth do dwell. . ." A laudable effort was made to suppress the snorts and sniggers' – because it was, of course, Psalm 100.

A call to his home congregation, Sixmilecross, was accepted and he was installed there on 20 April 1916. Later that year he married Miss Susan M'Kee of Belfast, who, for forty-three years, was his devoted wife. She was a charming hostess whose warm friendship and culinary expertise helped to make the manse a place where 'old friends may stretch out their legs and want to stay'. W.F., in earlier years, rode a motorcycle but, strangely, never drove a car, so Mrs Marshall acted as his chauffeur on all his preaching, fishing and social peregrinations.

Their elder son, the Rev Charles Marshall, MA, is minister of Ballyshannon and Donegal Presbyterian Churches. Margaret, their daughter, is a talented artist and a member of the Ulster Society of Women Artists. To her careful custody of her father's manuscripts we owe this compilation of his poems, and by her response to an increasing demand for their publication, at home and abroad, she has honoured his memory. John, the younger son, is a dental surgeon and Clerk of Kirk Session of Castlerock Presbyterian Church.

W.F. received a call to Castlerock, where he was installed on

4 May 1928. Though the panoramic view from the manse included the hills of Donegal, Lough Foyle and the North Atlantic, yet the splendour 'where the great seas roar along a northern strand', never erased the memories of his happy boyhood or the impressions of his earlier ministries in 'Old Tyrone'; of its friendly people, its wooded hills and its singing streams. These sparkle like jewels in 'Tullyneil' and could

> '. . . conjure pictures of the kind
> No canvas need retain,
> For I can paint them in my mind
> And live my youth again.'

His contribution to the life of the Church was recognised in 1952, when the Presbyterian Theological Faculty, Ireland, conferred on him the honorary degree of Doctor of Divinity.

His publications became more prolific in his Castlerock days. After *Verses from Tyrone* came *Ballads and Verses from Tyrone, Ballads from Tyrone* and *Tyrone Ballads*. All these, by their titles as well as their contents, show how his heart was warmed, his thoughts inspired and his speech moulded by Tyrone's rich and historic culture and the beauty of its natural features. Wherever he went his ear was always tuned to catch the expressive phrase. On greeting an old Castlerock gardener with a comment on the fine summer weather, he was greatly amused by the retort: 'Sure I min' Junes, if ye'd sput on a stane it wud' a bizzed.' He loved a turf fire and his order for a load of turf was sometimes delivered in verse.

Though this is a definitive collection of W.F.'s published poems, it also includes others which are personal poems to friends, to celebrate private family events.

His published work is not, of course, confined to poetry. A series of talks entitled *Ulster Speaks,* broadcast and later published by the BBC, justifies his proposition that 'dialects are not corruptions of English, as so many people seem to think. . . they are the roots of something that has taken centuries to grow and come to flower, and even that's not saying enough. They are the museum. . . of the most useful language in the world'.

The Rev W.F. Marshall was appointed Lecturer in Elocution at Magee University College in 1932, a post he was well equipped to fill because of his command of expressive language, his preaching experience and the tone and clarity of his own voice. From my student days our friendship, based on our common interests in the Church, fishing and rugby football, flourished through the years.

Ulster sails West: '*The story of the great emigration from Ulster to North America in the 18th Century, with an outline of the part played by Ulstermen in building the United States*' reveals the influence of Ulster-Scots in ecclesiastical, educational, legal and agricultural spheres. The lists of those with Ulster ancestry include, among others, the Rev Francis Makemie, father of American Presbyterianism, and Cyrus M'Cormick, inventor of the reaping machine; Samuel Morse, the pioneer of the electro-magnetic telegraph and the code that bears his name, in addition to Andrew 'Old Hickory' Jackson and Ulysses Grant, both of whom were Presidents of the Republic. This is a work of detailed research, accurate chronology and factual detail.

The Corduroy Bag is a three-act country kitchen comedy which, though the text is available, as yet remains unpublished. He also wrote a one-act play on the emigration from County Derry in the eighteenth century, and the founding of New Londonderry, New Hampshire, for incorporation in the Presbyterian Pageant. His version of Shakespeare's *A Midsummer Night's Dream* in Ulster dialect was broadcast by the BBC. The literary tragedy of his life was the fate that befell the manuscript of an Ulster dialect dictionary, almost completed, which was irretrievably mauled by his Golden Retriever pup. So W.F. assuaged his disappointment by writing *Planted by a River,* an historical novel set in Tyrone at the end of the seventeenth century, which was serialised by the BBC.

His research into the history of dialect and culture in Ulster was acknowledged by the Royal Irish Academy when he was elected to its membership in 1942 – his most valued literary distinction.

His Charger White is a richly and originally illustrated volume of his children's addresses in which, says St John Ervine, 'he speaks to children exactly as a kindly and understanding and instructive man should speak, neither condescending to his audience nor rising above its head'. What a pity that a volume of his sermons, so carefully prepared, so neatly written, so cogently preached, has not been published! A visitor to Castlerock Church, who knew of W.F.'s interest in fishing, said after a service, 'Mr Marshall, if you can fish as well as you can preach, God help the fish!' 'The highest compliment I was ever paid,' said W.F.

He was an ardent and accomplished fisherman – a youthful

interest he maintained through manhood. In later years, the days he spent fishing Lough Melvin and Lough Eske were sheer delight to him. Often, as he folded his tall frame into the front seat of the car, did we hear his Te Deum – 'Thank God for a good breakfast and the prospect of a day's fishing.'

Reference is made to his life-long interest in fishing in several poems, especially in 'Plus Ultra' and 'My House'. One day he handed me the rough manuscript of this latter poem and, a few weeks later, it appeared in the *Presbyterian Herald* over the nom de plume 'Tandragee'. To my enquiry as to why he had not appended his name he replied, 'You know that "Tandragee" means "Backside to the wind" – the way an animal stands when it is not well – that's just how I feel.' He bore his illness with the resolve, serenity and dignity that were characteristic of the man and of the faith he professed. In a letter he wrote to me at that time he said, 'The BBC want a series of reminiscences, but I can't settle myself to it. . . the old head floats from time to time, and the ticker takes an odd racing fit, and the anginas are as usual, but the form is not bad. . . Give us a surprise some evening. Yours, Bill.'

Declining health brought to an end a distinguished active ministry of over forty-one years, and he retired on 31 December 1954.

The BBC, shortly after his death, paid tribute to him in a recorded programme produced by John Boyd and introduced by his brother, Rev Professor R.L. Marshall, which included the reading of several of his poems. No eloquent epitaph could more accurately describe W.F. than his elegy on the Very Rev Dr William McKean in 'The Minister':

The speech so fragrant of the folk he served,
The steadfastness that made his friendships long;
The manful leadership that never swerved;
The kindness of the strong.

The human ways that chained him to his friends,
The humour hidden in the deep grave eyes;
The boyish zest in all a full life sends
Or lore of books supplies.

So the great spaces of his mind were sorted
With gear of wisdom garnered far and wide,
Till truth to fairer heights of beauty soared,
And God was glorified.

Grand vision of a glad new time was his
But, while it halted in the longsome years,
God swiftly called him from the life that is,
And crowned him with his peers.

'In one of his last poems,' says Rev Dr M.W. Dewar, 'the gem-like "Tullyneil", there is a recognition of the Gael, as well as a recollection of his own Plantation stock in Ulster. The sense of the past, blending with the present, was always strong within him whenever he wrote of "Tyrone among the bushes". . . Nostalgically, the dying poet looks back to the village school, where his father taught, and to the "Plain old house of God" where he and his are laid to rest.'

So on 27 January 1959, his Faith and Hope rewarded, he was laid to rest in his beloved Tyrone, in 'Tullyneil's embrace'.

It is to be hoped that this collection of poems, in so far as it is humanly possible to do so, makes the reader feel the warmth of his personality and his innate good nature.

J.A. Todd
Garvaghy
Banbridge

I wish to express my thanks to the following people for their generous help in preparing this volume of my father's poems for publication: Dr Dewar, Dr James Johnston, Mr James Moore, Mrs Daphne E. Moore, Mr Andrew Todd, and Dr Robert Ussher.

Margaret Marshall
April 1983

to every son and daughter of Tyrone
wherever you may be

PROEM

I do not hide behind my shield,
Nor send my challenge through the field;
This Muse of mine has not supplied
Sob-stuff about my own inside.

For while my song to you is known,
My soul, I trust, is still my own;
And wherefore not? A man may see
That God's great world is more than he.

IMMANUEL

I saw a star across the snow,
And it was big and bright and low,
As I lay out long years ago
    Upon the hills of Bethlehem.

I roused the shepherds in the fold,
For high in Heaven the joy-bells tolled,
And music, as from harps of gold,
    Stole down the wind to Bethlehem.

The shepherds rose, with startled cry,
For God had folded back the sky,
And hosts of angels, white and high,
    Were singing down to Bethlehem.

Fear not, for lo! good news we bring,
Glad news that makes the joy-bells ring,
For unto you is born a King
In David's town of Bethlehem.
So sing a song for Bethlehem!
Send out the word from Bethlehem,
To all mankind this word for them –
Immanuel in Bethlehem!

The star was low above the town,
It lit my feet as I ran down,
It sparkled like a jewelled crown,
    Above the inn at Bethlehem.

The quiet beasts were standing there,
And Joseph, stooped in loving care,
And Mother Mary, proud and fair,
    Beside the crib in Bethlehem.

I saw three kings come to the door,
Each lifted off the crown he wore,
And kneeled, and laid his gifts before
    The King of Kings in Bethlehem.

Now bend the knee, before Him fall,
The King and Saviour of us all!
Bow down beside the crib and stall
That cradled Christ in Bethlehem!
Sing loud the song of Bethlehem!
Send out the word from Bethlehem,
To all mankind this word for them –
Immanuel in Bethlehem!

A shepherd boy, in sheepskin clad,
Stepped forward, and his face was glad;
His joy was all the gift he had,
    A poor man's joy at Bethlehem.

Now kings that rule dominions wide,
And shepherds that in fields abide,
The rich and poor, still kneel beside
    The Lord of all in Bethlehem.

Come all ye children from your play,
And sing with me our carol gay,
Of Him Who came on Christmas Day,
    A little child to Bethlehem.

For God was good Who sent us here
His Love within a Baby dear;
O spread the story far and near,
That all may go to Bethlehem!
O sing the song of Bethlehem!
Send out the word from Bethlehem,
To all mankind this word for them –
Immanuel in Bethlehem!

CEILIDTH

It stopped my step on the hard flags,
    That verse of an Irish song,
Patrolman, you on your Broadway beat,
    I'm feared you're thinking long.

There's a low house, a thatched house,
    At the foot of Bantown Lane,
With a half-door, and a hearth fire,
    And a pot linked on a crane.

It's dayligone, when the stars peep,
    And the cans clink in the byre;
There'll be good crack when the lamp's lit,
    And the fir flames in the fire.

Better crack when the latch lifts,
    And the decent neighbour men
Make their kailey as like as not
    Till the wag is striking ten.

For life is quiet in old Tyrone,
    And the way of our world is slow,
And they kailey about from house to house
    As they used to, times ago.

And they're all friends at the fireside,
    Man of the house and all;
He rubs the twist in the heart of his hand,
    And tilts his chair at the wall.

And they all have share of the soda bread,
    And the strong tea in the bowls,
And maybe the night is a wild night,
    And the sleet spits on the coals.

And maybe the night is a fine night
    With a moon and a high sky;
But what's the odds on a short road
    Whether it's wet or dry?

So the door swings, and the half-door
  On the decent neighbour men,
And they get convoy to the county road
  As the wag is striking ten.

And the door's barred, and the fire raked,
  And the socks hung on the crane,
And the light dies in the low house
  At the foot of Bantown Lane.

THE FAIRY HILL

I know a green hill
   Near till a road,
It's green with the shamrock
   That no man sowed:
For the Shees sowed the shamrock
   An' brought the black bee
To make it grow for ever
   On the steep green lea.

There's a burn slides by it
   To the railroad line,
A slow burn by it
   – This hill of mine.
An', man, it's so shapely
   An' so green an' so roun',
Ye'd know it was the Wee Folk
   That set it on the groun'.

An' I know a good man,
   A good man an' true,
Who had it from his neighbour
   (A good man, too),
That just a half a year ago,
   Comin' from the mill,
He saw the fairies dancin'
   On this very hill.

Deed an' deed the same man
   Wouldn't tell a lie;
Sure he saw the Fiddler
   Cocked up high,
Sittin' on a benweed
   Near a crooked thorn;
Oh! that thing happened,
   As sure as you were born!

An' I know a good man,
   Wise as you or me,

An' he saw the Lochrie Man
    An' heard the Banshee.
So it's me for the Wee Folk,
    In troth they're livin' still,
The dacent Gentle People
    That made the Fairy Hill.

Rail an' road an' green hill,
    Odd neighbours you!
Tripper Folk an' Wee Folk,
    The Old an' the New.
Motors gallivantin'
    Past the Orange Hall,
Sure I wonder what the Wee Folk
    Think about it all.

THE BIG TROUT

I had a comrade,
  Barelegged Joe,
And we went fishing
  Long, long ago.
He came trotting
  A yard after me,
For I was a big chap
  And Barelegs wee.

Soon as ever I got
  Out on the street
I heard behind me
  Quick-running feet;
Barelegs coming
  Biting at a bun,
Flying down the Strand Brae
  Hop, skip and run.

Then, with the greenheart
  Swinging in his hand,
He followed me in trespass
  On three men's land,
Till streams low and hasty
  Rose bank-full
And deepened into silence
  In Soshy's Pool.

Down in the turnhole
  Lived a big trout,
Sometimes we saw him
  Walloping about.
Oh! he was a monster,
  More than a pound,
But crafty, crafty,
  We soon found.

An Olive and a Claret
  And a nice March Brown

And then two Daddies
    We floated down,
A minnow and a maggot,
    And after that
A big white fly
    And a wee black gnat.

Then we got fine gut
    And an old fly hook,
And, prone on the bank,
    With hands that shook,
We cocked big worms
    Before his nose
And the grub that you get
    Where a dockin' grows.

But he scorned them all,
    Artfully he
Just made a fool of us,
    Joe and me;
Till the tempter came
    And we sank very low,
And an evil deed
    I wrought with Joe.

Darkly we debated
    Our foul plot,
The horsehair line
    And the running knot.
'It's very, very wrong,'
    I whispered low,
'There's nobody about,'
    Said Barelegged Joe.

We pulled a cow's tail,
    Soon we had a snare
Fastened to the greenheart,
    But long cowhair
Dipt in the water
    Is soft like wool,

It lay against the rod-top
    And wouldn't open full.

Joe from his pocket
    Produced a fiddle-string,
Said I, 'Man, dear, Joe,
    That's the very thing.'
Then for the lassooing,
    Age-long it seemed,
'Pull, ye boy ye, pull now,'
    Wee Joe screamed.

Up to the heavens
    An old cap sped,
Barelegged Joe
    Was standing on his head.
Criminals – no matter,
    Let that pass,
Hadn't we a pounder
    Kicking on the grass?

The greenheart now
    Is a light split-cane,
Far bigger trout
    On the grass have lain,
And Joe's man-big
    And has men to rule,
But he minds about the trout
    In Soshy's pool.

God bless rivers
    Rattling in the sun,
God bless fishermen
    Every one.
And God be with the good days
    Long, long ago,
When I went fishing
    With Barelegged Joe.

GOORDASPORE
A Ballad of General John Nicholson

Lay me a wreath at the Kashmir Gate,
  And another in London town,
These – for the Two who saved a State
  In the year of red renown;
In the red, red year of the Ridge of Pain,
  Of murder, lust and spoil,
When Larens was comrade to Nicul-Sayn
  And Dungannon saluted Foyle.

Nicholson's Column is resting a while
  On the road to Goordaspore;
Never a halt for thirty mile
  And the men can march no more:
But the tardy bugle sounds at noon,
  And the Halt! is sweet to hear,
Nicholson's men they are sleeping soon
  But where is the Brigadier?

Mounted, motionless, scorning the shade,
  Nicholson sits in the sun,
His lips are tight, for the Column's delayed,
  There's a hot march still to be done!
The men are pillowed on dusty kits,
  But, out on the road before,
The Brigadier still on his charger sits
  With his face to Goordaspore.

And one wakes here, and another wakes there
  From the stupor Toil supplies,
And still, as each man stirs in his lair
  And opens his heavy eyes,
He nudges his neighbours one by one
  And shews them what he sees –
The Brigadier out in the pitiless sun
  On the road beyond the trees.

11

So man after man they wake, dead-beat
  And unrefreshed, but still
They pull themselves to their weary feet
  And curse, as warriors will.
But after the curse they lift a cheer
  For him who rides before,
And Forward! thunders the Brigadier
  On the road to Goordaspore.

There is fighting soon and skirmishing hot
  Or ever the Sepoys fled,
There is fighting enough at the Trummi Ghaut,
  And Nicholson's sword is red.
But the heart of Lawrence leaps care-free
  When he hears the fight is won,
'India hasn't a man,' says he,
  'Like our John Nicholson.'

And Lawrence says to the Brigadier
  In his quarters at Lahore,
'John Nicholson, though I need you here,
  It is Delhi needs you more.'
So Nicholson rode with a loosened rein
  On the last long ride of all,
From Goordaspore to the Ridge of Pain
  And the breach at the Kashmir wall.

Far from Foyle the Lawrences wait
  The Coming of God the Lord,
Nicholson sleeps at the Kashmir Gate,
  He has sheathed his mighty sword.
But the faith they kept lads learn to keep
  Through good report and ill,
As long as the silver Foyle runs deep,
  And Dungannon sits on the hill.

DUNMULLAN

There's a place they call Dunmullan
   Where my own folk used to be;
There's a farm down in Dunmullan
   That was Paradise to me:
For the Lord Who set His heaven
   In the clouds that hide His throne,
It was He that made Dunmullan
   In the County of Tyrone.

The Lord He made the Sperrin,
The heather hills of Sperrin,
The Lord He wrought in Sperrin
   Till He tired of heath and stone;
So then He came to Gortin,
Came up the road from Gortin,
And through the Gap of Gortin,
   To Dunmullan in Tyrone.

It was then He made Dunmullan
   In a pleasant fold of ground,
Oh! the hills – He made them homely,
   And He set them all around;
It was then He made a valley
   Where the hazels bloom in May,
And He filled it with the music
   Of the burn below the Brae.

Then He made for it a people,
   But for me He kept the best,
Kin of mine who sought His pleasure,
   Waiting for His promised rest.
So their sundown had no sadness,
   And no other place I've known
Held so many hearts as merry
   As Dunmullan in Tyrone.

A cart in harvest weather,
And three of us together,

We rode upon the tether
Where the yellow corn was mown:
Rebuke – 'twas idle dreaming,
And threats were only seeming,
For a pair of old folk, beaming,
Absolved us in Tyrone.

When the fields were white at Christmas
And the sun forsook the sky,
We went padding to Dunmullan
By the Low Road or the High:
There's a burn across the High Road,
Back to see it I must go
Some December when it bubbles
Down between its banks of snow.

On the Low Road fields of Farrest
Border still the honeyed moor;
Farrest winds are heather-scented,
Unforgotten their allure.
Ah! but sweetly – soft and sweetly,
Calling back the years out-grown
Blow the winds across Binyoran
At Dunmullan in Tyrone.

The sun has sunk behind me,
The darkness comes to find me
In search of spells that bind me
With a charm that's deeper grown;
I see the lights of Sperrin,
The lonely lights of Sperrin,
They're all I see of Sperrin
From that hill-top in Tyrone.

Sure I know that just a stranger
Sees no beauty there at all;
Sure I know it and forgive him
That his rapture is but small:
For the song my heart is singing
Strangers never heard it sung,

14

And the secret of Dunmullan,
    You must find it when you're young.

If you want to see Dunmullan,
    Stranger, lift your book of days,
Somewhere near its clean beginning
    There's a picture surely stays –
Home and kin, a dear old roof-tree,
    Stream and field and mountain lone,
Can't you see it? It's Dunmullan
    As I see it in Tyrone.

So set the pages spinning,
And, past the days of sinning,
If you turn to the beginning
    And your heart is not of stone,
The vision – you will see it,
Be thankful you can see it,
The same as I can see it,
    In my County of Tyrone.

SHANE MILL

There's a green glen hidden in the middle of Tyrone,
  There's a grey house sheltered by a hill,
And the glen runs along to a little bridge of stone,
  And the grey house stands beside a mill.
Now the mills are merry from the Lagan to the Foyle,
  As the millstones triumph o'er the grain,
But you'll hear the sweetest, as you travel to Dunmoyle,
  Humming near the bridge at Shane.

Oh! the whins are covered with the gold of May again,
  And the whitethorn blossom has begun;
There are blackbirds calling in the middle of the glen,
  And a wee burn singing in the sun.
But the best lies yonder in the shadow of the hill
  Where a wheel makes showers like the rain;
For I am the miller, and my sweetheart is the mill
  Humming near the bridge at Shane.

When my days are over, there's a boon I hope to win,
  – The good Lord will never say me nay –
I will hie me often to the valley in Cloghfin
  Where the breeze blows down from Cavanreagh.
I shall fling no shadow, though the sun may shine above,
  I shall leave no footprint in the lane,
But I'll miss no greeting if I hear the mill I love
  Humming near the bridge at Shane.

THE RIVER

There's a river in the country, and it's there I will be going,
  Though it's long since I have left it, I have fished it in my dreams;
Sure I'll soon be there to see it – even now I hear it flowing,
  The chatter of the shallows and the purl of little streams.

Back of there the sun is shining, and the riverside is cheery,
  There are gowans for a carpet, and the moss to make a throne;
I will rise and leave the city, for my heart is growing weary
  For the open meads of summer and the river in Tyrone.

I'll go home beside the river, and the cares will slink in hiding,
  And the years go rolling backward till they're out of sight and ken;
Home to see the silver pathway down between the meadows gliding,
  God be thanked, when I have seen it, I shall soon be young again!

Mirrored deep in glassy reaches, lucky bits of cloud are stealing,
  Nor at call of man or master will the vision speed away,
Till I leave the din behind me, and I hear the shriek of reeling
  By the pools of dark Remackin where the slender willows sway.

When the sun's behind the mountain, and the cottage lights are
      peeping,
  Shouldering the old portmanteau, I will take my staff in hand,
While the road winds dim before me, and the meadow mist comes
      creeping,
  And the magic of the gloaming folds around a silent land.

Then my heart will beat the faster, for another love enthralls me,
  Older than the lure of waters chuckling gaily into foam,
Just a light within a window, and an open door that calls me
  Down the quiet loanin' swiftly to the old folks and my home.

OUR SON

He was only a cub, big-eyed an' shy,
    When he travelled across the sea,
A sorry cub when he said good-bye
    To the hills of Athenree.
Trig an' dacent he went away,
    His fortune for to win,
With a good warm suit an' a muffler gay,
    An' a wee round trunk of tin.

But he landed back last Carmin fair
    In the gran'est Yankee clo'es,
His specs are sich as the Yankees wear,
    An' his chat comes down his nose.
An' he's big an' fat – though I mind him slim,
    With a waistcoat white an' smart,
An' behivins the luggage he brought with him
    Made the full of a donkey's cart.

The wife's from Clare – she was raired in soot,
    An' she scrubbed a Yankee floor,
But now she's nothing from head to foot
    But a jinglin' jooilry store,
Chains and bangles an' rings that shine,
    Buckles across her toes,
Rings in her ears – if the woman was mine
    I would turn a ring in her nose.

An' she's a woman likes soft to lie;
    How could she sleep on a shelf?
How could she wash herself, she'd cry,
    Except in a tub of delf?
Soup she wants, an' coffee, bedad,
    Liver an' bacon an' fish,
An' salad's a thing that must be had –
    Kale cut up in a dish.

So our son's at home, an' under his skin
    He's the very same to see

As the boy that carried his trunk of tin
  Down from Athenree.
Sure, he left in turf, an' fetched a go
  Of water the day he came,
But his mother an' me, the two of us know
  He'll niver be jist the same.

For, what do you think? the man would chew
  The bit goes intil her mouth,
An' the wee back room it wud niver do
  For the flipe that was raired in the South.
So he's taken a house with a bath an' a lawn
  An' marble clocks that strike,
An' he motors to see us off an' on,
  – *A kin' of a stranger, like.*

BERNISH GLEN

The sun's red rim
　　Is hidden soon,
The low clouds dim
　　The rising moon.
Shy badgers hide
　　Still in their den,
But rabbits glide
　　Through Bernish Glen.

The twilight blurs
　　Pool and morass,
No wind-breath stirs
　　The withered grass.
Across the Gap
　　There's light to see
A lone crow flap
　　To Athenree.

Here all is still,
　　But from the vale
Steals up the hill
　　A farm-hand's hail,
A faint far clink
　　Of can and tin
Where lanterns wink
　　Down in Cloghfin.

Wee folk, they say,
　　Skipped to and fro
Up Bernish way
　　Long years ago.
But fairy ring
　　And elf-shot cow
And pixie king
　　Are fool-talk now.

The greybeards rave
　　Of highwaymen,

And of a cave
    In Bernish Glen,
Of ghosts that wail
    Before the dawn,
– But that's a tale
    Of years long gone.

Yet if you were
    In grey moonlight
Alone up there,
    Perhaps you might
Just change your mind
    Like many men
And look behind
    In Bernish Glen.

THE HILLS OF HOME

The Lord bate back the rollin' sea,
An' made the worl' for you an' me;
He made a power of level lan'
At Portydown an' at Strabane;
An' then with heather, peat an' stone
He built the mountains of Tyrone.

So travel up, or travel down
You'll see them risin' all aroun';
There's wans in other parts, I've heered
That mortyal big that you're afeered;
But even when a man's his lone
The hills are frenly in Tyrone.

The Derryman, I hope, is proud
Of Sperrin tops that touch the cloud;
Still, when I see, behin' the barn
The big, brown back of Mullagharn,
I'd let him keep, while she's our own,
The whole jingbang outside Tyrone.

There's Bessy Bell, she rises steep,
You see her well from Cooley Sweep;
She wears a very purty crown
That's changin' now from blue till brown;
For looks, I'm certain sure there's noan
To bate big Bessy of Tyrone.

The rest are kin'ly, wee an' low,
Where you can hear the moorfowl crow;
There's glens among them, man, they're prime
For shilter in the winter time;
Forbye, when frost bites till the bone
There's piles of turf in dark Tyrone.

Ay, God was good made level lan'
At Portydown an' at Strabane;
But knowin' folk, He thought black shame
To make the country all the same:
An' so, with heather, peat an' stone,
He made the mountains for Tyrone.

PURPLE AND GOLD

Sun-lit prairies in the West land,
   Prairies golden with the wheat;
Glinting dimness in the West land
   Where the sky and prairie meet;
Yet the Motherland that bred me
   Fairer to my eyes has grown,
As the longsome years have led me
   Far and farther from Tyrone.

Long, long shadows o'er the Homeland,
   Silver webs on whins and broom;
Mists that veil the mountain Homeland,
   Darkening the heather bloom:
Softly from the hills of Derry
   Cooling winds across are blown,
And the sun that smites the prairie
   Throws a kiss to dark Tyrone.

Sunshine lords it in this lone land
   Where no kindly shadows fall;
I am weary for my own land
   And the song in spruces tall:
For Remackin sweetly flowing
   Through its arch of weathered stone,
For the homely gorse that's growing
   Round Drumsheeny in Tyrone.

Far away I hear you calling,
   Motherland! still dear to me;
When the autumn leaves are falling
   I'll be back across the sea,
Tramping through the mist that gathers
   Down from Sperrin's summits lone
To the homestead of my fathers
   On the uplands of Tyrone.

SUNDOWN AND TWILIGHT

The fields are lonely, and the land is still,
    The West is rosy with the dying sun;
Yon pillared smoke you see on Foremass hill
    Speaks of incoming when the work is done.

The silent trees that sentinel the tower
    Lift feathered tops beside its summit grey,
Nor stir a leaf, for sundown has its dower
    Of rest and peace till God shuts up the day.

But with the twilight, hark! the moors let go
    The swift, cloud-bringing and exultant breeze
That storms the stillness like a mortal foe,
    And shrieks its passage through the churchyard trees.

Now all is clamour. But my heart swings far,
    Searching, unbidden, till the years restore
Youth, and the riot of a harbour-bar
    Where springtides battled with a Western shore.

A LITTLE SHIP

A little ship at sunset left Lough Foyle,
    White ensign clear above the darkening tide;
Starlight flashed down on sailormen whose toil
    And vigil ceased, as for our life they died.

No stinging shame for loss of old renown
    Flushed on their faces at the last parade;
The ship sank slowly, and the men went down,
    Their trust unbroken, and their flag displayed.

Death leaped to meet them, and their thought of home,
    Of all they hoped for from the years to be,
Passed in the fury of the surface foam
    That crashed around them in the winter sea.

God be their portion! for their hearts were true,
    Who faced in every sea the creeping foe
To keep the Lordship of the ocean blue,
    Like Drake and Nelson in the long ago.

Suns shall not smite them, nor the winds assail,
    Long resting theirs, till time and tide are sped,
Till earth's last Dawn sends up her streamers pale,
    And all the seas give up an Empire's dead.

THE ROAD

The fronting miles are steep and very dreary,
Let me remember your undaunted soul:
Mine is the striving till the heart grows weary,
Yours the dull waiting till I reach the goal.

Yet, as I tread the highway of my sorrow,
Somewhat of solace shall my steps pursue,
And shape my dreams, until I count the morrow
Another milestone on the road to you.

For, while the way winds bleak and long before me,
'Tis not so lone but I shall see your face,
And feel your presence like a mantle o'er me,
Until you meet me at the resting place.

OVERHEARD

'It's all wrote down,' said Patrick,
  'What happens ivery day,
The stories they be tellin',
  The things that people say;
The chat at wakes an' weddin's,
  The thrade that's goin' on,
It's in a book,' said Patrick.
  'Yir a liar!' stuttered John.

Said Pat, 'The clargy praiched it
  As plain as plain cud be,
An' I don't see no raison
  Why you should liar me.'
'I'll let ye know the raison,'
  Said John, with scornful look,
'The best horse in yir counthry
  Cudn't dhra' the book.'

ABSENT

The Fairies never dance now,
   Their wee lamps are cold;
You never get the chance now
   To win a crock of gold;
The holy thorns are dead now,
   The Lochrie Man's a dream,
We've Santa Claus instead now,
   And gramophones and steam.

But you and I are old men,
   And sure we know that he
Who rides behind the reindeers
   Is not for you or me:
He only comes to see folk
   That want a top or ball,
But God be with the Wee Folk,
   They were for us all!

I'd never grudge the young men
   Toys to which they cling,
Teams that work at football,
   Bookies in the ring,
The swiping of the batmen
   Earning steady wage,
The bellowing of fat men
   Pranching on a stage.

I'd rather see a red coat
   Slipping down the Glen,
I'd rather hear the Fiddler
   And catch the Lochrie men,
I'd like the nights of May-time
   With Puca at his tricks,
When Fairies had their playtime
   Swinging caman sticks.

I used to see their foot-tracks
   Round the fairy-thorn,

29

I mind them in the moonlight
   Shearing at the corn.
Sure no one could deny them
   Their frolic and their joke,
And no one dare defy them.
   – Our own Wee Folk.

I think I hear the young men
   Give a big guffaw,
They think they are the wise ones
   Laying down the law.
But never mind such rude folk,
   Sticking out their tongue,
The Wee Folk were good folk
   When you and I were young.

Alas! that was long ago,
   The red coat's a clout,
The fairy fiddle's broken,
   And the wee lamps are out.
And all the gold is rust now,
   The merry feet are still,
The darkness hides the dust now
   Within an empty hill.

HERE AND THERE

Yesterday
We were storm-choked
And stung with spray,
Collar-soaked
On the green path;
Stooped to the rain
On a high shore,
And words were vain
With the wind's roar
And the sea's wrath.

But to-day
In the Glen of Fawns
The new-mown hay
Scents wee green lawns;
And sweet release
Is ours, in things
Fragant of home:
Here bindweed swings,
And slow beasts roam
Our Hills of Peace.

ME AN' ME DA

I'm livin' in Drumlister,
   An' I'm gettin very oul',
I have to wear an Indian bag
   To save me from the coul'.
The deil a man in this townlan'
   Wos claner raired nor me,
But I'm livin' in Drumlister
   In clabber to the knee.

Me da lived up in Carmin,
   An' kep' a sarvint boy;
His second wife wos very sharp,
   He birried her with joy:
Now she wos thin, her name was Flynn,
   She come from Cullentra,
An' if me shirt's a clatty shirt
   The man to blame's me da.

Consarnin' weemin, sure it wos
   A constant word of his,
'Keep far away from them that's thin,
   Their temper's aisy riz.'
Well, I knowed two I thought wud do,
   But still I had me fears,
So I kiffled back an' forrit
   Between the two, for years.

Wee Margit had no fortune
   But two rosy cheeks wud plaze;
The farm of lan' wos Bridget's,
   But she tuk the pock disayse:
An' Margit she wos very wee,
   An' Bridget she wos stout,
But her face wos like a gaol dure
   With the bowlts pulled out.

I'll tell no lie on Margit,
   She thought the worl' of me;

I'll tell the truth, me heart wud lep
   The sight of her to see.
But I wos slow, ye surely know,
   The raison of it now,
If I left her home from Carmin
   Me da wud rise a row.

So I swithered back an' forrit
   Till Margit got a man;
A fella come from Mullaslin
   An' left me jist the wan.
I mind the day she went away,
   I hid wan strucken hour,
An' cursed the wasp from Cullentra
   That made me da so sour.

But cryin' cures no trouble,
   To Bridget I went back,
An' faced her for it that night week
   Beside her own thurf-stack.
I axed her there, an' spoke her fair,
   The handy wife she'd make me,
I talked about the lan' that joined
   — Begob, she wudn't take me!

So I'm livin' in Drumlister,
   An' I'm gettin' very oul',
I creep to Carmin wanst a month
   To thry an' make me sowl:
The deil a man in this townlan'
   Wos claner raired nor me,
An' I'm dyin' in Drumlister
   In clabber to the knee.

A FAERIE LAND

There is a land where wise men find
 The simple joys of old,
Sweet-scented air and breezes fair
 And sunsets red and gold.
A faerie land of moor and mead
 From this world's tumult far,
And a silver sheen that splits the green
 Where pleasant waters are.

There are lucky streams that chatter by,
 And pools that swallows skim,
Where sunbeams dance, and shadows glance,
 And the cares of life grow dim;
And a magic wand in a faerie hand
 Dispels the fisher's woes,
And flies are right, and lines are tight,
 And the South wind always blows.

And some there be who thro' the years
 That faerie land have trod,
And long have seen its banks of green
 Where drooping willows nod;
From boyhood days have sung its praise,
 And afar have seen it shine,
Up from the brook and the bent pin-hook
 To the angler's rod and line.

Anglers all! they have heard the call
 To a land so fair to see,
They seek it still with a steady will
 Wherever they may be:
There fishers go when March winds blow,
 When summer suns are high,
And their hearts are gay in the autumn day
 As the leaves go sailing by.

Anglers all! they have heard the call,
 They have joyful captives been,

In boyhood drawn, they followed on
　　Through all the years between.
They follow on till the sun is set,
　　And youth and strength are past,
Till the light grows dim by the river brim,
　　And the line runs out at last.

SECRETS

The sun goes over behin' the hill,
  Over the hill an' down;
If I went slidin' along a beam
  I'd maybe reach the town.
She'll be up again in the mornin',
  Red, an' risin' fast;
If I was over on Tanderagee
  I'd catch her climbin' past.

The moon is hidin' in Bernish Glen,
  Hidin' the most of the day;
If I'd slip canny along the burn
  She'd not get far away.
May I never die, but I'll try it,
  An' roun' the worl' I'll brag
How I whammeld the moon in Bernish
  An' fetched her home in a bag.

ALMA MATER

On tides long ebbed drift back the things that were,
 Long thoughts of youth, when care was still to be,
And dear dead days, when friendship made life fair
 Beside the Western Sea.

The far-strayed memories come trooping home,
 Till, visioned clear beyond her girdling walls,
Stands Alma Mater, and on tower and dome
 The morning sunlight falls.

The scenes return – for greeting one by one;
 Youths at the sea-wall near the close of day;
The boats of Claddagh, dark against the sun,
 Spots on a silver bay;

The heights where D'Arcy dreamed upon the turf;
 Dim ghosts of Arran in the sun-mist clad;
Tramps in the starlight while the winter surf
 Foams at the promenade.

Grey Menlow towers, from Corrib rising sheer
 Greenness of beech, and white of trailing thorn;
And waves lap-lapping on a little pier,
 Upon an April morn;

The shabby rooms where fellowship was high;
 The seabirds calling on a moonlit shore;
The last June glimpse as town and tide swept by,
 Westward of Oranmore.

The best of memories, the friendship leal
 That lay between us in the pleasant years;
God will restore them when His times reveal
 The passing of all tears.

So in life's eve, down memory's long halls,
 Steal morning winds that on the spirit cast

The sweet enchantment ere the curtain falls
  Full on the sunny past.

Comes once again the thunder from the tower
  The old-world streets, the boats at Claddagh quay,
Rain from the West, and through the lifting shower
  The sunlight on the sea!

THE CHAIR

He said:
'John's off his head.
He slides a chair
Before his toes,
And everywhere
The creature goes
It's always there,
His chair.

One day,
They ran away,
This funny pair;
The warders laughed;
The chase was rare
Of John the Daft
Sliding with care
His chair.'

Poor John
Slowly passed on,
Grave-faced, to share
With fools and mad
Asylum fare;
Strange that I had
No mirth to spare
Just there!

For we
Are so foot-free.
No subtle snare
Can clog our feet,
No bondage fair,
No weakness sweet,
No hindering care,
No chair!

THE RELIEF

Carry me up the wall!
I can hear the guns begin;
My strength is spent, but I'll die content
If I see the ships come in;
If I see the ships come in
After the dreary wait,
And I hear the cheerful din
Down at the lower gate,
I will know that the worst is past,
Over beyond recall,
Ay, should I die on the rampart high,
Carry me up the wall!

This is the Sabbath day,
But, along from street to street,
From the belfry tall to the farthest wall
I can hear the cheering beat;
I can hear the cheering beat,
And my hope begins to blaze,
Hark to the running feet!
And the lifted psalm of praise!
But the tumult ebbs away,
Stilled are the ramparts broad,
For the ships are there, and the wind is fair,
And the issue rests with God.

We have eaten horse and dog,
We have fed on salted hides,
On the chickenweed and the aniseed
And nameless things besides;
On the nameless things besides
That are fattened on the slain,
On the slinking thing that glides
At sunset from the drain.
But the Famine fights us still,
And the Succours nothing dare,
And the fleet we cheered when it first appeared
Mocks at our long Despair.

Many a night I've seen
The lanterns on the spars
Swinging slow with a yellow glow
Beneath the quiet stars;
Beneath the quiet stars,
Till our trumpets tore the night
And we lifted back the bars
And sailed forth to fight:
To fight and forget the pain
In the stress of conflict sore
Till the sunlight shone in the cool June dawn
On the ships below Culmore.

Surely the bitterness
Of Death was overpast
When the dawnlight broke on the herded folk
Cowering in the blast;
Cowering in the blast,
They were flung like dogs to die,
Till we sent the message fast
And raised the gallows high;
But our dead lay all around us
Under the ramparts grim
Black be the shame on Rosen's name,
The Lord will deal with him!

Mark, comrades, how the ships
Sail steadfast for the port,
The guns ashore great salvoes pour
But the frigate blinds the fort;
The frigate blinds the fort
And leaves the food-ship room,
It is Death the sea-men court,
Red Death around the boom.
But alas! the lifted cheer
In long lament is drowned,
For the tide is slack, and, bounding back,
The ship is fast aground.

Aground, but vicious still
With unappeased desire,
For every port that fronts the fort
Is spitting smoke and fire;
Is spitting smoke and fire
While the boat that tows her mate
Dares now a passage dire
And a shore aflame with hate.
O God! Who art our Rock!
Our sure Defence and Stay!
Make bare Thine arm and shield from harm
These valiant few this day!

Praise to the God of Battles
For what mine eyes have seen!
They falter not for the splashing shot
But swing the axes keen;
They swing the axes keen
Till the cable parts in twain,
Hard on the oars they lean
And the food-ship moves again
Out from the shrouding smoke,
Spurning the logs of pine
While the wading kerne, left far astern,
Snarls at the Saxon swine.

Glory to God again!
For the ship that we espied
Before the boom with bows of doom
Lifts up her leaning side;
Lifts up her leaning side
As the low red sun sinks down,
Swims on the rising tide
And spreads her canvas brown.
Light now the dying beacon
Long flaming for our grief,
Ay, pile it high, for the ships are nigh,
The ships that bring Relief!

Never a night like this
Was seen by old or young;
Blithe are the feet that skim the street,
And the merry bells are rung;
And the merry bells are rung,
And the straining boatmen row
Till the ropes ashore are flung
And the vessels moored below;
And the tears are tears of joy,
And the cheering cleaves the sky,
And loud and long is the swelling song
Of praise to God, most high!

Carry me down the wall,
Take me home to my kin,
My strength is spent, but I die content,
I have seen the ships come in;
I have seen the ships come in,
It's the last of them I'll see,
For my head begins to spin
And my sight departs from me.
But oh! I am battle-weary,
I'll be glad when the bugles clear
Shall sound Release, Recall, and Peace,
Hold up! – 'Tis Roll-call – *Here!*

THE MINISTER

Remembrance journeyed with us all the way
    Down from his high place on the rain-swept hill,
Pursued us homeward in the ebbing day,
    And tarries with us still.

The speech, so fragrant of the folk he served;
    The steadfastness that made his friendships long;
The manful leadership that never swerved;
    The kindness of the strong;

The human ways that chained him to his friends;
    The humour hidden in the deep grave eyes;
The boyish zest in all a full life sends,
    Or lore of books supplies.

So the great spaces of his mind were sorted
    With gear of wisdom garnered far and wide,
Till truth to fairer heights of beauty soared,
    And God was glorified.

Grand vision of a glad new time was his,
    But while it halted in the longsome years,
God swiftly called him from the life that is,
    And crowned him with his peers.

There, on high reaches where the view is broad,
    Freed from the mists that lower landscapes mar,
He sees at last the whole intent of God
    In earth and sun and star.

THE FLAG

They raised it on the lone hillside,
  above the heather bloom,
While, down the glen, the cold grey dawn
  still wrestled with the gloom;
While o'er the heath-clad mountain tops
  the mists of morning rolled,
They spread their banner in the breeze –
  the Covenant flag of old.

They boldly bade defiance
  to the mitre and the crown,
For Christ was King and Priest among
  the hills of heather brown;
And, far from temples made with hands,
  no passing bell was tolled,
For those who made good ending
  for the Faith and Flag of old.

All through the bitter, dragging years,
  they fought their lonely fight,
They walked a way of darkness,
  but they glimpsed afar the light;
Endurance unto blood was theirs,
  and misery untold,
Until at last they triumphed
  in the mighty days of old.

For truth was more than coronets,
  and freedom more than gold,
When peer and peasant rode to war,
  and striplings' hearts were bold.
When, spite of stake and rack and chain,
  remained the dauntless few,
Who flashed the signal far and wide,
  'Fling out the folds of blue!'

'Fling out the broad blue banner!
  Let God the issues hold!
Beneath the war-torn folds renew
  the Covenant oath of old!
Yea, though with blood of us the heath
  be dyed a darker hue,
For Christ His Crown and Covenant!
  Fling out the folds of blue!'

JOHN THE LIAR

Ere yistherday I dhriv the mare an' cart
To Carrickmore, the Indian male was done;
An', coming forrit to the railway bridge,
I seen an oul' boy runnin' down the road.
'Twos John the Liar with his two han's up
To kep the mare; ye'd hear the gowls of him
For far enough: 'Get back!' sez he, 'Get back!'
I had to stap.
        Well, it was freezin' hard.
An' bitther cowl; an' min' ye I had play,
(Yon mare's the deil for gettin' on hir en':)
But there wos John, he had his two han's up,
Scared like an' peghin', with no hat or coat;
A man's unaisy when he sees the like.
'The Lord bliss me,' sez I, 'what's wrong?'
                          Sez he,
'Be gomentays, I went an' killed two pigs,
Ye niver seen the like of them two pigs,
Throth they wor tarra; jist the five months oul'.'
'The deil a hair I care,' sez I, 'ye killed
A score of pigs; stan' out the road!'
                          Sez he,
That solemn I wos scared, 'Howl back!
For God's sake will ye stap!' I stapped again;
An' he says up to me, 'I killed them pigs,
But when I had them scraped an' clane,
I seen I had no place to hing them up.
In or about the house there wos no bame
Near sthrong enough to kerry them two pigs.
Well then, I tuk a thought: I wheeled them here
An' hung them from the bridge. I got them down
This mornin' with enough to do; an' now
What with the weight of them thremenjus pigs
The arch is only hingin'?'
                    I wos mad,

Behevindhers ye niver seen a man
As mad as me: I near dhriv over him;
I whupped the mare an' tore across the bridge,
I think I hear him yit, his roars an' laughs,
The eedyit!
                I was worse nor him.

THE LAD

They were no great aff-set anywhere,
    The scutchers times ago,
For drink it follyd the most of them
    That wrought among the tow.
Plenishment they'd have little or noan
    Except for what they'd stale,
An' they'd make the childher go out an' beg
    Gowpins of oaten male.

I knowed a scutcher that wrought in Shane,
    He was a drunken scrub,
But he rared a son, an' I mind the son
    A smart wee lump of a cub.
His clo'es were wings, an' his cap was tore,
    An' his fire was the fire at the kill,
An' he went to school on his wee bare feet,
    An' niver got half his fill.

Above the mill was a quare big hill,
    He could see to the graveyard wall,
To the market-house, an' the station gates,
    An' the new Hibernian Hall.
You'd hear him singin' goan up the hill,
    But the dear knows why he sung,
For the people thought they would see the day
    When his da would sure be hung.

When the Twelfth was near he'd march the road,
    His drumsticks in his han',
Boys, he was prime at the double rowl
    On the lid of an oul' tin can.
He played his lone, for the other folk
    Were ashamed of him an' his rags,
So he thrinneld his hoop an' waded the burn
    An' ginneld for spricklybags.

I mind the year he took up with me,
    The ploughin' had just begun,

I'd watch him leadin' the horses roun',
    The dhrunken scutcher's son!
Little I thought that afterwards
    More than a son he'd be,
For his father died in a water-shough
    An' he come to live with me.

He was odd in a way; I think he heered
    What nobody else could hear,
An' he seen what I could never see,
    The more my sight was clear.
The top of a hill bewitched him still,
    An' the flame at the mountain's rim,
But a runnin' burn was the best of all
    For he sayed it sung till him.

There were some that went that far as to say
    He was sure to turn out wil',
But the wee lad grew till he grew man big
    An' kep the heart of a chile.
The longer he lived about the place
    The less I had to fear.
There was never a word from him to me
    But done me good to hear.

I'm feelin' oul' since he went away,
    An' my sight is gettin' dim;
I niver axed for to keep him back
    When they needed men like him.
He's sleepin' now where the poppies grow,
    In the coat that the bullets tore,
An' what's a wheen of medals to me
    When my own wee lad's no more?

RETURN

When the long dull day is done
   Hasting homeward I will go;
You are waiting for your son,
   And the hours are dragging slow
Bitter winds and driving rain
   Toss the tree-tops to and fro,
But the sun will shine again
   In your welcome – when I go.

You will meet me with a smile
   Flushing on your wrinkled face,
I will watch it for a while,
   Halting on my quickened pace.
Comrade cares will vanish far
   As I hear your greeting low,
And the Faith no Doubt can mar
   Fold around us – when I go.

THE SPEARS OF GOD

Behind the Sperrin where the sunsets die
   No streamers flaunt in crimson and in gold;
   The darkened ridge lifts up no outline bold
Against the glory of a Western sky;
For Gloaming came, while yet the stars were shy,
   And creeping mist along the valley rolled;
   The tree-tops shivered in a breeze grown cold,
And, in a smur of rain, the Night drew nigh.

Yet, ere the legions of the Night prevail,
   God, Who is Light, their perfect triumph mars;
For, in the murmur of the rising gale,
   The host of Heaven with the Darkness wars:
And the clouds are riven, and the sky grows pale
   Before the onslaught of the thrusting stars.

ON TULLYNEIL

It is my pleasure here to trace
The lines upon my Mother's face,
    To wait and feel
    Her sure appeal
In moor and mead and hill,
    To greet her rugged beauty
    And to lay my loving duty
At the feet of Her who bore me
Who is Mother to me still.

For here are joys that shall endure,
The fragrance of the purple moor,
    The bells of blue
    That blossom through
The greenness of the lint,
    The rain from Foremass clearing
    And the cottages appearing,
The little whitened cottages
With window-panes that glint.

The hedges robed in spring attire,
The gorse aflame with spring desire,
    The living breeze
    That bends the trees
Above the Glisha mouth,
    The 'Cut' like silver flowing,
    – I can see it, and I'm going,
For the big trout are leaping
And the wind is in the South.

Some joys wear out and such I know
Upon my rubbish heap I'll throw;
    But till I die
    My flag is high
Beside my Mother's throne:
    However time may test me,
    Or distance try to best me,
My shield is for Her service,
And my sword is for Tyrone.

SUNT LACHRYMAE RERUM

I was sitting one day
In cricket-time
(May),
In the 'Cage',
In a rage,
With a fly
In my eye,
And the tears
Dropping,
And the desk
Sopping.

And the Head came along
With his shoulders back,
And he stopped in his track,
And he said, 'What's wrong?'
And I said, 'Alack!
And Alas!
Alack!'

So he came quite near,
And he said, 'Well, now,
Will you let me hear
The why and the how
Of the tears
Dropping,
And the desk
Sopping,
And the sob,
And the sigh,
Why?'

Now what would you do,
With a cricket match due
And you
In a rage
In the 'Cage'
With a fly

In your eye
And the Head
By?

I cried
And I cried,
And I said,
'Dear Master,
I confess
These drops
I exude
Allude
To the lost props
Of Euclid,
Yes.'
Faster
The liquid
Down the desk-lid
Slid.

And what did he do,
The Head?
Well, he cried too,
He said
Boohoo!
And stroked my brow,
And breathed, 'Well now,'

And dried me down
With the tail of his gown,
And said,
'You're a credit,'
(Like that,
Out pat
He said it),
'A credit.'

Away I went,
Content,
For he planked me down

A half-a-crown
And leave to step
Up town,
Also
No
Prep.

No he didn't,
He didn't;
By a whole lot
He did not.
But he took my hand
And he waved a wand
And he warmed a part
That was not my heart,
And, as he flung
The wand aside,
He prophesied
With bitter tongue
I would be – hung.

THE ROYAL SCHOOL

There's an old grey mother in dark Tyrone
That we served in the years long gone,
But we left her side, for the world was wide,
And each to his place passed on:
And wherever we be, on land or sea,
There's a song that her lieges sing,
For our mother's name is a Royal name,
And her gold was the gift of a King.

For her heart is young, but her fame is old,
For it's many a year ago
Since the dower came, and the Royal name,
And the stainless shield we show:
Oh, her years are long, but her hand is strong,
And her eye like an eagle's still,
And she trains her brood as a mother should
Till they hark to her wholesome will.

In the quiet night, when the lamp is low,
We are back in the steep old town,
Where our Mother waits by her open gates
For the lads that wear her crown:
And the sterner things that manhood brings,
They fade like the passing foam,
We are boys again with the boy's heart then
As she bids us welcome home.

So the belted sword, and the parson's coat,
The wig and the fresh M.B. –
We part with them at her garment's hem,
Just our Mother's sons are we.
And the King we'll greet, as is only meet,
With a cheer that is deep and full,
But the song we'll sing till the rafters ring
Is the song of the good old school.

R.S.D.: A SCHOOL BALLAD

Sing the good old shanty, boys, wherever you may go,
Sing of crown and castle and an ancient date below,
Sing it with a chorus, so that all the world may know
We learned the holy Latin in Dungannon.

> Hurrah! Hurrah! Dungannon wears the crown,
> Hurrah! Hurrah! the castle and the crown,
> When Derry was a village and Belfast a little town,
> We learned the holy Latin in Dungannon.

James the First of England sat in purple on his throne
When a dusty postboy brought the message from Tyrone
From his loyal planters who were making woeful moan
And craved the holy Latin in Dungannon.

Up arose our Lord the King and by his crown he swore,
'Lands shall be their portion and of treasure goodly store,
So my faithful servants shall endure this grief no more,
I'll send the holy Latin to Dungannon.

'They'll wear Dungannon's castle with a crown above,
   to show
I 'stablish it forever as a Royal School, and so
My citizens will bless me, and their little sons will go
And learn the holy Latin in Dungannon.

'Matrons I will send them to attend their little wants,
Little beds to sleep in, so my Royal pleasure grants,
And masters, very worshipful, to dust the little pants
And teach the holy Latin in Dungannon.

'By and by they'll bigger be, and learn to play the game,
To fight their battle fairly, which is the noblest fame,
And into men she'll mould them, and all her sons will
   claim
There's more than holy Latin in Dungannon.'

Years have fled – three hundred, we've a shield
   without a stain,
R.S.D. for ever! sing with all your might and main,
Lift it now, boys, lift it till he hears it – Niculsayn,
Who learned the holy Latin in Dungannon.

Glory to the good old school beside Dungannon town!
Glory to the noble king, and fair be his renown!
And glory everlasting be with all who wore her crown
And learned the holy Latin in Dungannon.

CUSHENDALL

I dreamed of a sounding sea,
And a winding glen grown broad,
And the streams that run to the rising sun
Down from the hills of God;
And I thought I saw Glen-an,
And the Bally-e-mon Fall,
And it seemed to me they were good to see
But the best was Cushendall.

I dreamed of a sun-lit shore
Where the rose-bay willows grow,
Where the sound of the breeze in the village trees
Was a murmur soft and low;
Of the towers of Sorley Boy,
And Martin's ruined hall,
And it seemed to me they were good to see,
But not like Cushendall.

I dreamed of the hills of God
Where the sun goes down to rest,
Of a golden tongue and a sword well-swung
On Lurigédan's crest;
And I saw the drifted snow
On Trostan's mighty wall,
And I liked it well but not so well
As the lights of Cushendall.

I woke and I went my way
To the toil that waits for men,
But the sun-lit shore I would see no more
Till the stars came out again;
And the night brought back to me
The curlew's lonely call,
And the little bay on a by-gone day
With the sun on Cushendall.

BAD LUCK

The more he's so tarrible civil
McFadden's an unlucky divil;
Ye'll not have his animal long with ye
Till ye fin' that it's sure to go wrong with ye;
It's sartin to turn out a bad 'un,
The baste that ye buy from McFadden.

Do ye know what I'm tellin' ye, Sammy,
For the thruth is the best? sez oul' Tammy,
If 'twos only his duck ye wor buyin',
Do ye know what herself wud be thryin'?
In what water wud har'ly go roun' herself
She wud dook her head down an' wud drown herself.

OUR TOWN

Sometimes in the darkness I dream
   Of the town that is home to me still,
Of the gardens that slope to a stream,
   And the roofs on the side of a hill,
Of the town where the slow waters steal
   Underneath a half-circle of stone
At the foot of the hill of O'Neill
   In the middle of County Tyrone.

Very old, with the wisdom of years
Very sweet to the folk that she rears,
   Far away though I be
   There's a picture I see
And night after night it appears;
Oh! the hill of O'Neill is her throne,
And it's there that she mothers her own,
   Where the heather is near,
   And the river runs clear
By the greatest wee town in Tyrone.

Our town she is old, very old,
   But a good share of children has she,
Some toil in the city for gold,
   And some are far over the sea;
And some who love neighbourly ways
   And to walk in the paths they have known
Are content just to live out their days
   In our town in the County Tyrone.

This town can remember the years
   When O'Neill kissed the hand of a Queen;
All the welter of blood and of tears
   In the backgone the old town has seen.
And they say, in the far long ago
   In her midst rose a symbol in stone,
So the houses that clustered below
   They were christened the Cross in Tyrone.

They are many the old town has bred,
  And kindly her thoughts on them fall;
I can see them, the living and dead,
  And Maguire is the king of them all.
I can see Jack O'Neill and Mad Pat
  And old Mac just as deaf as a stone,
And Jamie who wore the tall hat
  And danced on our street in Tyrone.

Joe Orneil with the bill-hook who slew
  And reported the slaughter with calm;
Big Totty – a bit of a shrew;
  Mary Ann who was jealous of Sam;
And McCool with the tins in his kit,
  And the Cub – to three score he would own,
And old Phil with the humour that bit,
  – Sure, they're all from our town in Tyrone.

And they're all in my dream – to my joy,
  And to me it's a dream that is fair,
Of the street where I played as a boy,
  And the neighbourly folk living there;
The Market House hill where we sleighed,
  Tullyneil with its whins overgrown,
All the old-fashioned games that we played
  In our town in the County Tyrone.

A big moon is shining I know,
  On the old Market House in the trees;
There are shadows along the Cross Row,
  And golden panes gleaming through these.
But the golden lights fade – to my loss,
  And I wake in the darkness, alone,
But I still have my dream of the Cross,
  This dream of our town in Tyrone.

DUNGANNON ROYAL SCHOOL
1914–18

Lo! on their graves the kindly dews will fall,
The grasses spring, and flaming poppies nod;
The long sleep theirs, until the last loud call
Peals from the trump of God!

Mine is their fame, and what is mine is yours,
Therefore your tribute at my feet is laid,
That, while the fabric of my house endures,
Their glory shall not fade.

So that, in later days, my sons shall see
I held them dear who dared the scathe of war,
From Flanders fields to lone Gallipoli,
And spread my pride afar.

In girdled Kut, and Baghdad's desert ways,
And West! where Jesus walked in Galilee,
By burning lands where Sinai's sunsets blaze,
And Suez herds the sea.

For faith well kept in hunger, mud and cold,
For Peace now purchased at a bitter price,
By every memory that was yours of old,
Salute their sacrifice.

High in enduring stone your tribute set,
That in my house their names may still abide,
And grave in gold a mother's proud regret,
Here by her own hearth-side.

THE TWAIN

They were Twain when they crossed the sea,
    And often their folk had warred;
But side by side on the ramparts wide
    They cheered as the gates were barred:
And they cheered as they passed their King
    To the ford that daunted none,
For, field or wall, it was each for all
    When the Lord had made them One.

Thistle and Rose, they twined them close
    When their fathers crossed the sea,
And they dyed them red, the live and the dead,
    In the land where the lint grows free;
Where the blue-starred lint grows free,
    Here in the Northern sun,
Till His way was plain, He led the Twain,
    And He forged them into One.

And they grew in strength as the years went by,
    And the travail of Empire came,
And they went them forth to the ends of earth
    With the flag of ancient fame;
Till round the world, that flag unfurled
    Pursued the circling sun,
While foremost still when the day went ill
    Were the Twain whom God made One.

Up-lifted high, that flag will fly
    Above the Ulster-born
They'll hold it dear, and guard it here,
    Unmoved by threat or scorn.
And keep the Gate, despite dictate,
    As did the Twain made One,
And undismayed at the Last Parade,
    Fall in and hear 'Well Done!'

A COUNTRY

Often in twilight's sweet release I go
To seek a country that is fair to me,
Fairest in springtime when the hillsides glow
With broom and whin, and white of hawthorn tree:
Thither I hasten when the route lies free,
Straight as an arrow winging in the blue,
Home to my haven when the heart is low,
Home to my country where the dreams come true.

My ship of dreams will voyage Southward Ho!
Steal from her moorings by the silent quay,
Borne, like a bird, upon her wings of snow,
On to the haven where I fain would be.
Southward and Westward! till at last I see
The woods of Termon and the lighter hue
Of that green valley where the hazels grow
Down in my country where the dreams come true.

L'ENVOI

Friend, if your dreaming lacks its former glow,
And life's hot noon has lost its morning dew,
Pray that your eventide at last may know
Some sun-lit country where the dreams come true.

THE BALLAD OF CONGO

I've met with some travellers could draw a long bow,
With home-coming Yankees that bravely could crow,
With anglers in earnest and jarveys in jest,
But of artists in lying old Congo's the best.

Old Congo we call him, his name is Maguire,
With his head in the clouds and his feet in the mire,
With so much of the best and his share of the worst,
And all his life long an unquenchable thirst.

Old Congo has wit like the thrust of a spear
And a flaming abuse that is awesome to hear,
But dull is the heart that could fail to be stirred
By the magic he wraps round a phrase or a word.

His stories are marvels of fancy and wit,
He has genius to pick out the phrase that will fit,
And he lifts a big brush, and with artistry bright
He splashes his canvas with colour and light.

Far back in his youth for New York he was bound,
He stayed a few weeks and just staggered around;
In the hold of a steamer he stoked his way home,
The first and the last time for Congo to roam.

But this little episode's quite in the shade,
Beside the long journeys he says he has made;
You might take them for truth, but the truth is far fled
From the journeys that Congo has made, in his head.

Sure the tale of his shipwreck would make your flesh
    creep,
Of his hair-breadth escapes, and his nights in the deep,
Of the African sun, and the Labrador snow,
Of cannibals, pirates, and wee Esquimaux.

He can tell you of Mexico stories as true
As the tales that he tells of his life in Peru,

And he'll paint you a picture you'll never forget
Of the beards of the Lhamas in distant Thibet.

'Three weeks in New York I lay under a bed,'
But he knows more about it than ever you read,
From Barnum's big Circus to Tammany Ring
And the way to get smoking your pipe in Sing Sing.

But there's this about Congo, a fact I deplore,
To set out on his travels he needs less or more
Of something to oil him – a bucket or two
Of poteen or blowhard or petrol will do.

His legs have got feeble, his body's a wreck,
He has smashed every bone, as he says, but his neck,
And he tells us, and maybe he's not so far wrong,
That under the daisies he'll girn before long.

Then the nights will be silent, no more he'll let loose
The lightning retort, or the loud-tongued abuse,
Or that lurid and long-drawn-out sentence he hurls
At James of the Gateway or Kate with the curls.

As for James of the Gateway he'll bother his head
No more about beef, he'll sleep sound in his bed;
But sometimes I think he'll be tempted to say
The street's very lonely since Congo's away.

Oh! the light of our judgment is broken and dim,
So we'll not judge at all, we will leave it to Him;
For the God Who made Congo does nothing in haste,
And He knows – He knows to what purpose this waste.

DERVAGHROY

All down the road to Dervaghroy
   The fields are cold and bare;
A heavy sky shuts out the sun,
   And bitter is the air:
Death rides before us in a hearse,
   A creaking hearse and pair.

Death rides before us: all around
   The world is black and grey,
Save for the yellow chest that holds
   The silent, lifeless clay,
The flaring thing of brass and pine
   That leads the long array.

The land lies draped in black and grey;
   No bud is to be seen;
Upon the meadows by the road
   No blade of grass is green;
The matted tufts are bleaching now
   Where fragrant swathes had been.

Yonder – 'tis desolate as death,
   The corn grew up breast-high,
The home of merry myriad lives
   That swarmed in hot July;
Gone with the sheaves – by autumn driven
   To fold their wings and die.

* * * *

Slow through the village, and we reach
   The Laragh road at last;
The bare trees bowing by the road
   No kindly shelter cast;
But each bewails its nakedness
   And sighs for summer past.

Down by the low cross-roads you feel
  The bitter biting sting
Of icy wind, the wind that lifts
  The heather and the ling;
It sweeps along the black bog-pools
  And makes the willows swing.

Before the gates of Dervaghroy
  We leave the crawling Ford,
And, over yonder, call on God,
  And hear His name adored;
Soon, in the shadow of His house,
  Dust is to dust restored.

Hark! how the wind that meets the firs
  Their long low tribute frees;
The leaves that strew the tombs obey
  The bidding of the breeze;
They drift upon the busy spades,
  And flutter round the trees.

* * * *

The hearse goes rumbling back, for now
  The grave-grass hides the loam;
The standing horses make a stir,
  Their jingling bits afoam;
We board the waiting car and take
  The sharp left turn for home.

The racing clouds are higher far,
  The sky seems higher too,
And, looking up, you plainly see
  A little patch of blue,
With silver border where the light
  Behind is shining through.

The blue patch widens with the wind;
  The beaten clouds that run
Before the breeze are ript aside

And, through the entrance won,
Ablaze with victory there sweeps
    The round triumphant sun.

The folk that rattle down the road
    Fling greetings to and fro;
The engine hums a merry tune,
    Down Laragh hill we go,
The sunlight falls on Tullyneil
    And on the roofs below.

* * * *

Nothing is here for deep despair,
    Or death-bells sadly tolled,
This withered world shall live again,
    And bud and leaf unfold,
And golden corn in God's good time
    Redeem the black bare mould.

Our home is here; we have a life,
    'Tis filled with light and shade
But no thick darkness need oppress
    The world that God has made:
For we can rest our hope in Him,
    And never be afraid.

Darkness and Storm are Princes high,
    With Lordship far and wide,
But He is King and Lord of Lords
    Who never yet denied
His Bow of Promise on the Cloud,
    His Light at Eventide.

PLUS ULTRA

There might be something – find it! more than fun
     In throwing flies across Remackin trout;
A man went trailing asses once, my son,
     And found a sceptre as he tramped about.

Seven men were sad because the Lord had died,
     But Peter said, a-fishing I will go,
And, down along the pebbled waterside,
     The Lord Himself was walking to and fro.

Life lacking sweet surprises is a fraud
     That stops at giving you your selfish wish;
I say, my son, just buy yourself a rod,
     Take my advice, 'tis Peter's, go and fish.

SARAH ANN

I'll change me way of goin', for me head is gettin' grey,
I'm tormented washin' dishes, an' makin' dhraps o' tay;
The kitchen's like a midden, an' the parlour's like a sty,
There's half a fut of clabber on the street outby:
I'll go down agane the morra on me kailey to the Cross
For I'll hif to get a wumman, or the place'll go to loss.

I've fothered all the kettle, an' there's nothin' afther that
But clockin' roun' the ashes wi' an oul Tom cat;
Me very ears is bizzin' from the time I light the lamp,
An' the place is like a graveyard, bar the mare wud give a stamp,
So often I be thinkin' an' conthrivin' for a plan
Of how to make the match agane with Robert's Sarah Ann.

I used to make wee Robert's of a Sunday afther prayers,
– Sarah Ann wud fetch the taypot to the parlour up the stairs;
An' wance a week for sartin I'd be chappin' at the dure,
There wosn't wan wud open it but her, ye may be sure;
An' then – for all wos goin' well – I got a neighbour man
An' tuk him down to spake for me, an' ax for Sarah Ann.

Did ye iver know wee Robert? Well, he's nothin' but a wart,
A nearbegone oul' divil with a wee black heart,
A crooked, crabbit crathur that bees neither well nor sick,
Girnin' in the chimley corner, or goan happin' on a stick;
Sure ye min' the girl for hirin' that went shoutin' thro' the fair,
'I wunthered in wee Robert's, I can summer anywhere.'

But all the same wee Robert has a shap an' farm o' lan',
Ye'd think he'd do it dacent when it come to Sarah Ann;
She bid me ax a hundther'd, an' we worked him up an' down,
The deil a hate he'd give her but a cow an' twenty poun';
I pushed for twenty more forbye to help to build a byre,
But ye might as well be talkin' to the stone behin' the fire.

So says I till John, me neighbour, 'Sure we're only lossin' time,
Jist let him keep his mollye, I can do without her prime,
Jist let him keep his daughther, the hungry-lukin' nur,

There's jist as chancy weemin, in the countryside as her.'
Man, he let a big thravalley, an' he sent us both – ye know,
But Sarah busted cryin', for she seen we maned till go.

Ay she fell till the cryin', for ye know she isn't young,
She's nearly past her market, but she's civil with her tongue.
That's half a year or thereaways, an' here I'm sittin' yit,
I'll change me way of goin', ay I'll do it while I'm fit,
She's a snug well-doin' wumman, no betther in Tyrone,
An' down I'll go the morra, for I'm far too long me lone.

The night the win' is risin', an' it's comin' on to sleet,
It's spittin' down the chimley on the greeshig at me feet,
It's whisslin' at the windy, an' it's roarin' roun' the barn,
There'll be piles of snow the morra on more than Mullagharn;
But I'm for tacklin' Sarah Ann; no matter if the snow
Is iverywhere shebowin'; when the morra comes I'll go.

THE RUNAWAY
a sequel to 'Sarah Ann'

I towl yez afore about marryin',
   How the notion come intil me head:
I wos livin' in dhurt an' amdasbut,
   I wos pushioned with tay an' white bread.
I wos puddlin' at shirts in a bucket,
   I wos baffled with sarvints an' fowl,
An' wan night with me feet in the ashes
   I rusted – I did, be me sowl.

Sarah Ann, shure yez heerd about her too,
   But yez didn't hear more nor the half;
She's a fessend oul' thing, but her father,
   Wee Robert, he's tarble well-aff.
But, boys, when I mentioned the fortune,
   Ye'd a thought when the argymint riz
That he hadn't the nails for to scratch with,
   He's as mane as get-out, so he is.

Well, he cooled in the skin he got hot in,
   He got lave, the crooked oul' cowlt,
No falt till his daughter, I left her
   But I foun' meself still in a howlt.
Sure the bread that I baked wos like concrete,
   An' the butther – now I wud consate,
The man that can ate his own butther
   There's nawthin' that man cudn't ate.

I'd a litther of pigs to sit up wi',
   An' pigs is like Christens – man, dear,
Ye'd a thought they wor sthrivin' to tell me
   'We're lost for a wumman up here.'
Calves died on me, too, in the spring-time,
   The kettle got foundered in rain,
Hens clocked, or they tuk the disordher,
   An' me heart warmed till Sarah agane.

So I went, an' if Robert wos hasky,
    Sarah Ann wos as nice as cud be,
She done well, for who wud she get now?
    Deil a wan if she didn't get me.
But her father had still lik a coolness,
    Not wan word of welkim he dhrapt,
Nor he niver sayed what he wud give her,
    He wos dotin', she sayed – he wos apt!

I got full in the June fair of Carmin,
    I rid home, an' I met Sarah Ann
– The thurf wos near ridy for clampin'
    An' a wumman can give a good han' –
Sez I, 'Wull ye come for a half-wan?
    Ye'll not. Well, listen to this.
Yon hirplin' gazaybo, yir father,
    He'll say nether ay, naw nor yis.'

So sez I, 'I'll not stan' it no longer,
    Ye can take me or lave me, an' min'
Here's the cowlt can take me in the seddle,
    With you an' yir bardhix behin'.
So come on now, or stan' there for iver,
    Come on now, quet scratchin' yir chin,
It's a runaway, that's what we'll make it,
    Till Tamson's up there in Cloghfin.'

Sure I knowed she wud come, sure I knowed it,
    Is it hir? Boys, she just made a bowlt,
Got a shawl an' whusked it about her,
    Got stredlegs behin' on the cowlt.
Ay, stredlegs, for that's the way weemin
    Bees ridin' the horses all now;
But heth, 'twos an odd-lukin' runaway,
    For the cowlt had to wak like a cow.

Owl Tamson wos gled for to see us,
    An' dacent, he done what wos right,
He sent for the dhrink an' the neighbours,
    We had dancin' an' tay the whole night.

We got dhrunk, an' we fell till the fightin',
　　Be me sang oul' John's purty tyugh,
It wos prime how he leathered all roun' him
　　An' him jist as full as a shugh.

Big Jim ketched a howlt o' me whuskers,
　　Sez I, 'Ye can thry yirself, Jim,'
But me bowl Sarah Ann with a potstick
　　She soon lef' hir thrademark on him.
'Ye unsignified ghost!' sez his mother,
　　An' with that jist before he cud wink
She ketched Sarah Ann be the thrapple
　　An' whammeld her right in the sink.

When weemin gets wicked they're tarra,
　　Ye'll not intherfair if yir wise,
For ten townlan's wudn't settle
　　The birl that two weemin can rise.
It wos nearly been that up in Tamson's,
　　We fought from the fire till the dure,
We fought – if ye'd say it wos fightin',
　　We fought in a heap on the flure.

That an' all we got grate afore mornin',
　　We wor frens throughother ye see;
John yocked just afther wir brekwis,
　　An' we shtarted for Robert's, iz three.
But we niver thought what we wor in for,
　　Heth naw, we dhriv up at a throt,
But the welkim wos sharp, 'twos a pitchfork,
　　An' that's all the welkim we got.

Boys ye niver seen sichin a han'lin',
　　I wos thunnersthruck watchin' the birl,
The oul' da limpin' out wi' the pitchfork,
　　An' the frens makin' glam for the girl.
They dhregged her out over the tailboard,
　　She scramed, but I darn't intherfair,
An' they sliped her – aw lominty father,
　　They sliped her right in to the stair.

The gowls of wee Robert wos tarra,
   The veins riz like coards on his skull,
'How dare ye? How dar ye? How dar ye?
   I'll take ye to coort, so I wull.'
He miscalled me for all the oul' thurfmen,
   All iver ye heerd he went through,
Sez I, 'Ye may go till the bad place,
   I'm as good jist as she is, or you.'

An' sez I, 'Me oul' boy, yir as ignornt
   As a pig let loose in a fair,'
Oul' Tamson broke in an' he toul' him
   He cudn't fetch guts till a bear.
Well, boys, he wos frothin' with anger,
   The spittles flew from him a parch,
But what good wos that? We wor done for,
   We just had to lave him, an' march.

I come home. I sot down in the kitchen,
   Thinks I, 'I'll go through with it now,'
So I riz an' went back till oul' Tamson's,
   (He wos puttin' a ring in the sow)
An' sez I, 'I've a five naggin bottle,
   Put a coat on ye, John, it's like rain,
Iz two'll go up to Long Francy's
   An' tell him I'll take Liza Jane.'

Sez he, 'Ye've no call to be hasty,'
   Sez I, 'Aw yis I hev call,
When the bizz gets out through the country,
   I'll not get a wumman at all.'
Sez he, 'Liza Jane — who wud she be?'
'The fat wan,' sez I, 'she can plough,'
'Be me sowl,' sez oul' John, 'It's a tarra,
   But no matther, I'll go with ye now.'

So that's how I got me big wumman,
   We settled it quick, so we did,
I'm content, she's a brave civil crathur,
   An' quate, an' diz what she's bid.

Not hard to keep up – that's a good thing
    When times isn't good on the lan',
She's young, but she's settled, an' more too,
    She can work in the bog like a man.

She has no backspangs in her ether,
    No harm in her more nor a hen,
If I take maybe wan or two half-wans
    She niver gets up on her en'.
Sarah Ann now can hannel a potstick,
    If that's any affset – a mane,
Takin' wan thing jist with the other,
    I'm thankful I picked Liza Jane.

SAINT PETER

Saint Peter was a fisher, and
  'Twas what he liked to be,
But still he didn't understand
  His art like you or me.
He sunk his net – it's in the books –
  And lifted fish in shoals,
He towed them in with mighty hooks
  And roasted them on coals.

He's learned a lot, I dare avow,
  These nineteen hundred years,
No big seahooks for Peter now,
  No handlines, nets or spears.
In gentle Walton he confides,
  (Our Izaak's learning too)
And hosts of Izaak's sons besides
  Have told him what to do.

He kilts his coat – (above, I think,
  His apostolic knees) –
Gives Andrew with a saintly wink
  In charge the shining keys;
And speeds, light-hearted as a lad,
  With reel and line and rod,
To float his fly where streams make glad
  The city of our God.

THE WAY

Across wastes wild and barren,
　　Steering by sun and star,
A man set out from Harran
　　And journeyed fast and far,
Because Jahweh Elohim
　　Bade him leave home and kin
For a land that He would shew him,
　　– So doth the tale begin.

The man lived long, possessing
　　This promise of the Lord,
That in his seed great blessing
　　For all mankind was stored;
Believed through all wayfaring
　　In no god but in One,
Ay, thought that He, uncaring,
　　Willed him to slay his son.

In age and peering blindness
　　The son of that son died,
Whose sons by Pharaoh's kindness
　　In Egypt multiplied,
And grew while thus befriended
　　So rich in lands and gear
That Pharaoh's hand descended
　　At last on them in fear.

Hard burdens, Israel bore them
　　With shortened sobbing breath,
They shrank from whips that tore them,
　　Longed for the ease of death;
Till a voice for God like thunder
　　Cried, 'Let my people go!'
And plague and sign and wonder
　　Avenged King Pharaoh's 'No!'

Flushed babes in Egypt sleeping
　　Paled in their cots and died,

That land was filled with weeping
  To humble one man's pride.
The first-born, son or daughter,
  From sea to desert rim,
God doomed them to the slaughter,
  And Israel worshipped Him.

Free, Israel toiled through mountains
  That lift their snows aloft,
Halted by desert fountains,
  Sinned and repented oft,
Obeyed and disobeyed Him,
  And in that desert grim
With flowing curtains made Him
  A tabernacle dim.

With manna white He fed him,
  And with His own right hand
And holy arm He led them
  Into the promised land.
And there they builded altars
  And set the wood aflame,
Dragged up dumb beasts with halters
  And called upon His name.

Short shrift they gave to Baal,
  For Ehud God raised up,
And Ehud slew, and Jael
  Who gave her guest the cup.
There Jepthah's child was martyred
  To keep a vow profane,
Agag by Samuel quartered,
  And Uzzah swiftly slain.

There blood on altars rotted,
  Blood dript from cruel knives,
Red blood their garments spotted
  Who lived proud priestly lives.
There thick smoke rolled unceasing
  Above King David's hill

From altars wrath-appeasing,
　For such was Jahweh's will.

Seers whom no priest anointed
　Proclaimed from God the Lord,
'New moons and feasts appointed
　Are by My soul abhorred.
I'm full of lamb's flesh smoking
　And fat of beasts long-fed,
Bullocks in death-pain choking,
　And goats' blood streaming red.'

The sour priests said, 'These dreamers
　Contemn God's holy law,'
And stoned them for blasphemers,
　And scourged them red and raw,
And flung them from the city,
　And stroked their beards and prayed
To Him Who had no pity,
　– The God themselves had made.

Then on that night of killing
　The long-sought rosedawn streamed,
One came at last, fulfilling
　The best the seers had dreamed.
With Him no banners flying,
　No hedge of lifted spears,
But an infant's first soft crying
　And a mother's happy tears.

God's bells in heaven were ringing
　On that night long ago,
And God's white angels singing,
　And God's great star aglow,
And, round a straw-lined manger,
　God's beasts with ransomed lives
Had soft eyes for the Stranger
　Who had no priests with knives.

He lived and loved His mother
    And had His bread to gain;
With those who called Him brother
    He handled saw and plane,
And wrought with axe and hammer,
    And found life sweet and good
In a workshop's cheery clamour
    And the sharp clean smell of wood.

Down through the green fields striding
    He passed the lilies gay,
He saw where safe in hiding
    The little foxes lay.
He stood and watched the sparrows,
    The birds His father fed,
That hopped behind the harrows
    And perched above the shed.

Then went out, unrepining,
    The sons of men to call,
And oh, His face was shining
    With Love for one and all:
And knaves forgot their cunning,
    And vice her painted charms,
And little ones came running
    To be lifted in His arms.

They felt His grace restore them
    Who hearkened to His word,
They saw unveiled before them
    The beauty of the Lord.
He gave His Bread to feed them,
    He named Himself their Friend,
He pledged His word to lead them
    And love them to the end.

When men were hoarse with brawling,
    When hands were swift to smite,
When priests defiled their calling
    With perjury and spite,

His voice came softly stealing,
    'Come unto me and rest,
Lo! in My House of Healing
    Is room for every guest.'

'Were all your trials doubled,
    Though sore your sorrows be,
Let not your heart be troubled,
    Look up and trust in Me.
My presence shall attend you,
    My peace shall stay your mind,
And this good news I send you
    Shall be for all mankind.'

No scribe or priest or prelate
    But scorned the glad good news;
With what face dare He tell it
    That God loved more than Jews!
And, though with welcome fitting
    The mob Hosannas roared,
They turned from Him with spitting,
    – The King Who wore no sword.

They came and seized Him, flouting
    Their Saviour's Royal claim,
They filled the Court with shouting,
    These fierce-eyed sons of shame;
They stepped from altars gory
    A beggar prince to see,
– *But it was the Lord of Glory*
    They nailed upon the tree.

> *The long, long road from Harran*
>   *Ends not beside the hill,*
> *Across lands waste and barren*
>   *That highway windeth still.*
> *Not dim-lit since Messiah,*
>   *Clear, shining, safe and broad,*
> *But One road from Moriah*
>   *Through Calvary to God.*

A PARTING

Oh, your heart is stout,
An' I think me lad
You'll suffer a pile
An' larn at the rear
That you're just goin' out
On your kailey, bedad,
All the wee while
That you have to be here.

For it's feedin' on dust
The worl' to chase,
To sthravag about
An' have far till roam,
An' larn that you're just
In a lodgin' place
When the fire goes out
An' you have to go home.

IN TENEBRIS

Now, while the mist still hides the day,
And many walk in fear,
Lead Thou us through the shadows grey,
Until the road is clear;
Our fathers faced a toilsome way,
Let us not falter here.

End and beginning, each to Thee
Is as a tale long told;
Teach us the best is yet to be,
Whate'er the years unfold:
Dimness or sun, grant us to see
This far-borne gleam of gold.

Our Fathers sowed where we have reaped,
They sowed in blood and tears;
In wide-eyed faith their vision leaped
Down through the dim-lit years;
Content, if sacrifice high-heaped
Left us no room for fears.

So faith shall bid our doubts begone,
And all our fear subdue;
The happy peace, the fight long-drawn
Alike shall find us true;
The sunshine shall succeed the dawn;
We shall have naught to rue.

VALE

'I go the way that all must go,
   It has no fears for me;
Fearless I go, because I know
   That yonder I shall be
Where all my old-time comrades wait
   In a shining company.

'In pastures green no battles rage,
   But blossoms shyly hide,
And where the King's broad acres lie
   I shall be satisfied.

'The river ripples at my feet,
   The city gleams afar,
The sunset bell will tinkle soon
   To greet the evening star:
Across the shadowed ford I hear
   Far voices that I know;
The dimness lifts, and rising clear
The battlements of Heaven appear,
   The golden trumpets blow.

'The good knights wait without the gate
   To bid me to the board;
To-night I'll meet my Captain there,
   And render up my sword.
I'll sup in New Jerusalem
   When I have passed the ford.'

The bells were ringing vesper chimes
   In the church above the hill,
But now they ceased their chiming sweet,
   And all was very still.
The music of the birds was hushed,
   And through the woodland fair
No noise of rustling leaves was made,
The very tree-tops seemed afraid
   To mar the stillness there.

Then while the stillness stiller grew
   There came the last grey fight;
He wandered in the shadow land
   That borders faith from sight,
And passed along the road that leads
   Up to the gates of Light.

So underneath the silent oaks,
   While shades of gloaming-tide
Stole through the trees, he found at last
   The rest that life denied,
His dented helm upon his head,
   His long sword by his side.

D'ARCY'S POINT

The sea laps at the red sun's rim
    Out where the islands lie,
Bodeful of dusk, when Clare is dim,
    And Claddagh boats steal by.
Faintly I hear the wind-borne plaint
    Of inland trees afar,
A rattle as of blocks that slip
And drowsy voices from the ship
    That lies outside the bar.

The tide creeps up in ebb and flow,
    And still the tall cliff-side
Spurns in disdain the depths below
    Where restless sea-weeds glide;
Stands undismayed, while, foot by foot,
    The lurking shadows grow,
Until the mantling dusk drops down
And tiny lights in Galway town
    Begin to wink and glow.

Behind the hills a yellow moon
    Moves up to light me home;
The cobbled walk will riot soon
    In protest to the foam:
Now he who walks abroad may see,
    Beneath the pale moon-beams,
The White Queen wring her fingers gaunt,
Or D'Arcy's ghost flit by to haunt
    The high place of his dreams.

MARY OF DUNMULLAN

Away down in Dunmullan,
    One morning long ago,
You met me in a meadow,
    Where I was hired to mow;
And no words passed between us,
    But what the world might hear.
Yet Heaven's gates were opened
    When first I saw my dear.

Oh Mary of Dunmullan,
    The Lord was good to me,
Who sent you in the sunshine,
    My own true love to be.

Down yonder in Dunmullan,
    On that good summer morn,
Your eyes were like lint blossom,
    Your hair was like the corn;
Now all that gold is silver,
    But still undimmed there lies,
The blue of lint in blossom,
    Deep in your dear old eyes.

The green fields of Dunmullan
    Are scented still in June,
The burn is still as bonnie,
    And keeps its quiet tune;
God bless the day you met me,
    And gave your promise true.
And God bless dear Dunmullan,
    Dunmullan – me – and you!

TETHERED

They armed me out this afternoon in May
     To see the world; and I was glad to go,
     For all I'd seen of this year's passing show
Was from my bedroom window, as I lay
Week after week, day after longsome day.
     How lovely then to feel the soft wind blow
     On this high terrace, and to see the glow
And flash of flowers that keep my garden gay!

Lovely indeed, but less than my desire;
My vain desire! because the path is steep
And how should I return? I must not tire
Myself by climbing, must be sure to keep
On level ground, nor any further dare
Than this short journey to my terrace chair.

COMIN' HOME

There's a boy across the sea, an' he's comin' back to me,
An' I'll meet him down the loanin' comin' home;
I'll be countin' every day till the weeks have rolled away,
An' I meet him down the loanin' comin' home.
    Comin' home,
    Comin' home,
    So far away from me an' comin' home;
    Sure I know he's thinkin' long, but his heart will sing a song
    When I meet him down the loanin' comin' home.

Oh it's long an' long before, I'll be listenin' in the door,
But I'll meet him down the loanin' comin' home;
I'll forget the longsome years an' the loneliness an' tears,
    Comin' home,
    Comin' home,
    So far away from me an' comin' home;
    He's my love across the sea, an' he's comin' back to me,
    An' I'll meet him down the loanin' comin' home.

SEVEN

Six ducks went down the lane;
'Ducks is funny,' says Robert's Jane.

Says I, 'Funny, what do ye mane?'
'The way they wiggle,' says Robert's Jane.

Robert's Jane walked through the fair.
'It's very funny,' says Tom Adair.

Says I, 'Funny, what do ye mane?'
'To watch,' says he, 'the wiggles of Jane.'

KATIE

When I was young an' hasty
    I had all the say
An' oh but I was tasty
    In me dickey every day.
I had me ma to care me,
    I kep' a man to plough,
But Katie couldn't bear me,
    She has to bear me now.

They thought that they would rear her
    Modest-like an' quate,
She was a holy terror,
    An' often she was bate.
The rod was niver off her,
    Her legs were hammered red
But when her da would cuff her
    This is what she said.

What are ye batein' me for, da?
    Batein's for wans that's wee.
That I may niver stir, da,
    Batein' no good till me.

Katie couldn't bear me,
    Banged me up and down,
Troth she didn't spare me
    A snubbin or a frown.
That was only part of her,
    Only for a blind;
Deep in the heart of her
    She wanted to be kind.

THE LAKE

There's a lake that lies in Leitrim,
    in Fermanagh and in Leitrim,
A little lake in Leitrim
    at the edge of Donegal;
Oh! Melvin is the name of it,
    and far and wide the fame of it,
The lake below the mountain,
    with the fleet of islands tall.

The lake below the mountain
    has a call-sign on the mountain,
Humps and hollows on the mountain
    – man! you want to lift a cheer
When far away you spy them,
    for tomorrow you'll be nigh them,
Drifting down the rushes
    where the mountain side is near.

Slowly down the rushes
    in the breeze that sways the rushes,
There are rings along the rushes
    as the boat is stealing by;
And should you think of shifting
    where there's always lucky drifting.
The sannachan at Rosses
    will be flashing at the fly.

They'll be flashing there at Rosses;
    out beyond the stones at Rosses,
Oh! you'll drift the boat to Rosses
    while the breeze is fresh and free;
And later, since the rest of it
    might even be the best of it,
You'll search the Sunken Island
    as you're homing to the quay.

Ah! but on the Sunken Island,
 when a gale is on the Island,
Blowing hard across the Island,
 you might founder in the spray;
Better shun the road to Rosses,
 and the risk of spills and tosses,
And go down the Fir Plantation
 to the peace of Johnston's Bay.

Yet even the Plantation,
 the rocky-shored Plantation,
The long wind-swept Plantation,
 can be fraught with peril too;
Better far the road to Dolan's,
 you can board a boat at Dolan's,
And cruise among the islands
 for the golden gillaroo.

Fine to cruise among the islands,
 in between the bays and islands,
The tall tree-covered islands,
 and the bays that bend the shore:
But maybe for the sannachan,
 the fierce and fighting sannachan,
You'll set an Olive bobbing
 on the stormy deep once more.

For Straddle-bug or Olive,
 green or gold or sooty Olive,
A Claret and an Olive
 and a Butcher you may try,
And it might be brave and chancy
 to affix a Watson's Fancy,
But what's the use of prating
 to a man about a fly?

Ay! what's the use of prating?
    and forbye the storm's abating,
The sunset calm is coming,
    and the boat has lost its sway,

And the rise has gone completely,
    but the car is humming sweetly;
Board it, Angler, for McGovern's,
    and call this day a dav

TYRONE JIGS

Oh the Ironman came with a sword and a spear
    And the edge of his iron to carve him a throne,
And the words of the Ironman stay with us here
    For he christened the places in County Tyrone.
So wherever you go from Killoon to Corboe
    They are tuneful and sweet as a bird on a bough:
They set your feet tapping and tempt you to clapping,
    Oh stranger, just hark to the lilt of them now!

There's Cavanamara and dark Derrymeen,
    There's Carrickatane and Munderrydoe,
With Strawletterdallan and Cavankilgreen
    All dancing a jig with Cregganconroe.
Oh there's Curraghmacall and Bomacatall
    And Mullaghshantullagh and bright Gorticrum,
While merrily tripping and up and down dipping
    Are Sanaghanroe and Fernaghandrum.

        Sanaghanroe and Fernaghandrum,
        Where is the like from the Moy to the Plum?
        A fiddler could play it, a lilter could hum
        Sanaghanroe and Fernaghandrum!

There's Altmacossy and Croshballinree,
    There's bonnie Dunmullan and Edintiloan,
And Tullyodonell and Tanderagee
    With Tattynagole and Derrykintone.
There's Termonamongan and Tullynashane
    And – merry as ever and light on the toe
Here they come dancing in rhythm entrancing –
    Fernaghandrum and Sanaghanroe.

        Fernaghandrum and Sanaghanroe,
        Hark to the lilt of them! see how they go!
        Say them out loud or whisper them low,
        Fernaghandrum and Sanaghanroe!

Yet if you would fetch me to Sanaghanroe
Or Fernaghandrum, I confess
I'd be eager to see them and happy to go,
But for reasons I'll leave you to guess,
I would rather be back in the streams of Remackin,
Or knee-deep in Bernish in bracken and fern,
Or tramping the heather in warm August weather,
The grouse-haunted heather on high Fallaghearn.

Oh! high are the hills in the heart of Tyrone,
But the one I know best has a charm of its own;
Green Hill of O'Neill that my boyhood has known
My heart is with you in the heart of Tyrone.

For a cool wind is blowing on Tullyneil hill,
And the flags on the church are unfurled,
And a man could be over on Tullyneil hill
The happiest man in the world.
He could sit on the slope where it lies to the sun,
Or in shade where the crab-apples grow,
And prefer it to farming in places as charming
As Fernaghandrum or Sanaghanroe.

Come all ye Tyrone men of honour and fame,
The end of my song is a truth that you know;
You may travel afar, but there's always a name
That has charm and enchantment wherever you go:
For it's tied up with joy that was yours as a boy,
It is flesh of your flesh and was bred in your bone,
It's your Fernaghandrum and your Sanaghanroe
And your Hill of O'Neill in your County Tyrone.

VERSES WRITTEN BY UNCLE BILL TO DEIRDRE
in a book given to her in 1956

Deirdre, you asked your Uncle Bill
To write something. He said 'I will,'
But words like Deirdre give him bother,
They will not rhyme with any other.
And so he has to give it up,
And simply write 'My dear Miss Thrupp.'

WHEN NONNIE LOST HER DENTURES – 1953

Granny's lost her teeth,
Where did she set them?
Upstairs or downstairs
She can't get them.

Granny takes her food now,
How does she do it?
Hard toast and bacon,
She can't chew it.

Granny isn't tearful,
Granny's very cheerful.
Soon they'll present her
With a lower denture.
Molar and incisor
And the one that makes you wiser;
Gratis, too, gratis,
And I'll tell you how that is.
Her gums are nearly bitten through
But boldly she has written to
The Hospitals' Authority.
Now she'll get tomorrow tea
As soon as she's waken
And hard toast and bacon.

ON SEEING A CINE-FILM OF DEIRDRE
BATHING IN PENANG, 1953

The Major who went out to slay a
Lot of the Reds in Malaya
Has sent us a film of his daughter
Swimming about in salt water.

I reckon this beautiful picture
Was taken just after you'd kicked your
Knickers and sandals and socks off,
And hardly could wait till the frock's off.

(That last line changes the tenses.
But anyway, grammar no sense is;
And even it's not said politely,
The line that I wrote will do rightly).

Well, the film containing the photo,
Good Noel displayed it in toto,
(Dear me! You'll forgive me the Latin,
I was stuck for a rhyme and put that in).

Yes, Deirdre it was in the water
Swimming about like an otter,
Splashing and washing to get off
The nasty and clammy old sweat off.

Now what did they say and they do who
Saw it, old Boris and Poo-Poo?
Lassie and Quacky and Fluffy,
Blushing at you in your buffy!

Well Boris said 'Bow-wow,'
And Lassie bow-wow'd back,
And the brown duck said 'Quack-quack.'
And Fluff began to purr,
And may I never stir
But the Googooloos
Stood on their toes

And made wee springs
And flapped their wings
And crowed and crowed
As if they knowed
That there shown up
Was Deirdre Thrupp.

(On 'crowed' or 'crew'
I've pondered long,
But I should have knew
That 'knowed' was wrong).

OF SUCH IS THE KINGDOM

'O Mother! up in heaven do kiddies play,
Or go to school, or mitch, or run away?
Or have they just to sit upon a cloud,
And play a big melodeon all the day?

It's never dark up there, the preacher said,
There are no cots, you have a cloud instead,
How do they sleep, and not fall off the cloud?
How do they know the time to go to bed?

O Mother! would the holy angels scold,
If, only once, we just lay down and rolled?
Or fished with pin-hooks from the river-bank?
Or made mud pies upon the streets of gold?'

Here wept the child. O such a tearful flood!
The vision froze the anxious mother's blood.
'O Mother! if in Heaven the streets are gold,
We can't make pies there, 'cos there is no mud!'

THE TALKING FLEA

I knowed a man in the mountain,
    An' afore he dug the spuds
He coorted a great big woman
    With sweets an' cinnamon buds.
The man was as thin as a harra,
    He could live on the latch of a dure,
The woman, the more she was sonsy,
    Was light of her fut on a flure.

But the man knowed what he was doin'
    When he coorted Rosie MacDade,
For she was a useful woman
    With a powerful lep on a spade.
She was gran' with a grape on a midden,
    She could run the legs aff a foal,
Oh, she was the fit for a farmer
    In a place like Crockathole.

The man got married on Rosie
    An' fetched her home on a car,
He lit the lamp in the kitchen
    For the place was as black as tar;
He went out for to fother the cattle,
    But boys! a say! a say!
When he landed in from the byre
    Rosie was clane away.

The man (by name he was Daniel)
    Fell till an' cried like a wane;
He knowed the Fairies had Rosie
    An' how would he get her again?
I declare, the full of a piggin
    Wouldn't howl the tears he shed,
An' dismal it was for to see him
    Creep till his lonely bed.

But he wasn't long in the blankets
    Till he feeled the bite of a flay.

He clapped his han' in his oxter
      An' boys! a say! a say!
When he catched the flay till kill it
      He nearly died of the fright,
For it sayed, 'Now Dan, excuse me!
      You're squeezin' me too tight.'

'Holy Saint Patrick! what are ye?
      Baste or Christyin?' says Dan,
'Well indeed,' it says, 'I'm a Christyin,
      So plaze let me out of your han',
Sit up in the bed, ye boy ye,
      An' hap yourself in the rug,
An' open your thumb an' your finger
      An' let me light on your lug.'

Dan sat up in the blankets,
      An' boys! a say! a say!
He didn't know where he was sittin',
      He was trimmlin' for fear of the flay.
'Come, come,' it sayed, 'Be manly:
      I'm kinely, the more I'm wee,
Surely I'm not that scaresome
      An unsignified thing like me.

'I was turned till a flay by the Fairies,
      The King himself done the job,
Me that was raired to be clanely,
      An' me with rheumatics begob!
But the more I'm fatagued with the happin'
      – So far in the dark an' the rain –
I come wan's erran' to tell ye
      The way till get Rosie again.'

Be me sowl when he heerd about Rosie
      Dan pitched the blankets away,
He bounced out of bed like a lion,
      An' boys! a say! a say!
'Mister, Sir,' says he, 'your honour,
      If Rosie me darlin' was back,
The longest day that we're livin'
      The divil a flay will we crack.'

107

'Well Daniel, that's more nor dacent,'
    The craythir says in his ear,
'But I'm comin' straight from Rosie,
    She's livin', she's well, an' she's near;
She's in under a grassy mullan
    That rises in Carrigeen bog,
With a cannivaun bed to lie on
    An' aitin' the best of prog.

'Now, on Halla-eve night the Fairies
    When the moon begins to shine
Have a cammons match at Foremass,
    An' they'll not lave her behine.
She'll be comin' with them ridin'
    On a cowlt as white as snow,
An' the Fairies be to be dancin',
    So she'll have to travel slow.

'Now there's your chance, ye boy ye,
    When they're dancin' past the lane,
Be sure an' raych for Rosie,
    An' pull your might and main.
Stick both your arms about her
    An' lace them till they lock,
An' howl her, Daniel, howl her,
    Howl her till twelve o'clock.

'But don't, for God's sake, name it
    To man or baste or bird,
The Fairies, she sayed, would kill her
    If they joobed she had sent ye word.'
That was all from the insect
    But boys! a say! a say!
Wasn't Daniel glad to hear it,
    That nice discoorse from the flay?

'Mister, Sir,' says he, 'you can tell her
    I'll not say a word to a sowl,
An' if I get a howlt of Rosie
    In troth that howlt I'll howl!

108

An' see now, if ye would take it,
　　I'd bestow ye the half of the farm;
But the full of your mouth for supper
　　Ye can have it here on me arm!'

Then the flay, with a feed in him, happed it
　　An' Dan had a fortnight to wait.
But I'll warrant ye he went brave an' early
　　Down the wee lane to the gate,
An' there on the stroke of eleven
　　His sonsy big Rosie he seen,
With Fairies before an' behine her
　　An' her cocked up like a Queen.

Brave Dan made the glam for his Rose
　　An' that's what started the fun,
Ye niver seen sich a han'lin'
　　Since iver your day begun.
He lapped his arms about Rosie,
　　He bunneled her aff the cowlt,
An' ivery trick they could think of
　　They tried, but he hel' his howlt.

Well the Fairies went ragin' roun' them,
　　An' the King of them gave a squeal
An' turned her intil a salmon,
　　An' then from that till an eel;
He turned her intil a grey-houn',
　　An' he turned her intil a duck,
But no matter how he turned her
　　The howlt was niver bruck.

He turned her intil a bone-fire,
　　An' boys! a say! a say!
It was hard for Dan to howl her
　　An' her still bleezin' away!
But he locked his arms about her,
　　An' cursed them hilt an' helve,
An' the blissin' of God was with him,
　　For he hel' his howlt till twelve.

109

An' the minute the clock had struck it,
    The cowlt begun till jog,
The routerie riz an' hooked it
    Back to Carrigeen Bog.
An' Dan was left with his Rosie
    Oh boys! a say! a say!
He had somethin' in at his oxter
    Better far nor a flay!

Well that's the story of Rosie,
    The woman the Fairies stole,
An' the story of Dan, the farmer
    That lived in Crockathole.
But here! – if he kep his promise
    To that wee talkin' flay,
The two of them had some scratchin'
    Oh boys! a say! a say!

THE DRUMNAKILLY DIVIL

I met a girl in Beragh an' she said her name was Sarah,
　　An' I thought she was as fair a lass as iver wore a shoe;
So I went an' sat beside her, an' with tay an' buns supplied her,
　　An' to soften her I tried her with a lossenger or two.

Then later I got bolder an' I nipped her on the shoulder,
　　O I nipped her an' I told her I would take her on my knee;
But she said, 'You'll be in bother, for I'll go an' tell me mother,
　　I'll go home an' tell me mother if you're impident to me.'

But she said it with a twinkle, an' a brow without a wrinkle,
　　An' her laugh was like a tinkle that invited laughin' back;
So I started to provoke her, an' to hug her an' to poke her,
　　Till she vowed that I would choke her, an' her stays
　　　　began to crack.

Says I, 'Now don't be silly, I've a farm in Drumnakilly,
　　An' the more it may be hilly, there's a handy bit of bog,
We'll be happy there together with a bullock in the heather,
　　An' the goat upon the tether an' the donkey an' the dog.'

Then it wasn't long we tarried till the two of us were married,
　　An' home the donkey carried us – the presents made a load,
An' on them Sarah sittin' with a clocker an' a kitten,
　　As we jingled like a flittin' up the Drumnakilly road.

But the night was gettin' chilly when we come to Drumnakilly,
　　I could hear the bleats of Lily as the graith come off the ass;
Says I, 'I'll get a bucket, for I dunno how she stuck it.'
　　So I lifted wan an' tuk it up to Lily in the grass.

Well, the goat was very willin', an' the bucket bravely fillin',
　　But the milk was nearly spillin' when I heered an awful
　　　　squeal,
An' then there come a clatter over stones an' lyin' water,
　　It was Sarah on the batter up the loanin' to the fiel'.

She was leppin' like a lion an' her petticoats was flyin',
   She was roarin', she was cryin' fit to waken up the dead;
O she come without delayin', an' between the gowls an'
     prayin',
   I made out that she was sayin', 'John, the Divil's in the bed!'

I run in to see the Divil with a mind to spake him civil,
   An' behold ye Sarah's Divil was a hairy oul' buck goat,
With a smell for human noses that was anything but roses,
   An' a beard on him like Moses an' a dickey at his throat.

Says I, 'Me neighbour Micky must have done it, for he's tricky.'
   But a goat that wears a dickey is a goat I can't abide,
An' because a man that smelled him would incline to do it
     seldom.
   I cut the ropes that held him an' I chased the buck outside.

O sometimes me an' Sarah dresses up an' goes to Beragh,
   But she'll niver let me wear a dacent dickey like the rest,
An' the thing that is uncivil is to mention Sarah's Divil,
   The Drumnakilly Divil with the dickey on his chest.

MY HOUSE

I'd like a house that was my own
Beside a river in Tyrone;
The river at my garden wall,
    – When I've said that, I've said it all.
    I've said it all, and it's a dream
That has no substance, hope, or gleam,
Yet, now I'm old and on the shelf,
I talk about it to myself.

A little house, not hard to run,
With one big room to hold the sun;
A good turf fire to keep it warm,
Pictures and books to give it charm,
And easy chairs where old friends may
Stretch out their legs and want to stay.
    And want to stay – so there would be
A few spare bedrooms, two or three,
Electric current – lots of plugs,
And water piped – no bedroom jugs.
    All this within, but for a treat,
Outside I'd like a summer seat;
A sheltered place where I can go
No matter how the wind might blow.
    I'd like a garden full of bloom,
But here and there it must have room
For strawberries and apple trees,
And useful things like spuds and peas.
    I'd like a view, although I fear
It's hard to be provided here.
I'd like a mountain, lifted high,
And heather-clad to please my eye.
That mountain, friends, beyond a doubt,
I simply will not do without.
    And then just to complete my dream,
I'd like two fields along the stream;
A field above, and one below,
With open banks where one could throw
A cast of flies, if not with ease,

At least with skill, below the trees.
For (mark me!) trees I must provide,
But they'll be on the farther side.

     Above my house I'd like to see
The water flowing fast and free,
But not too deep for one to wade
Below a stretch the bushes shade,
And there entice a fish to rise
And take its pick of three wet flies.

     The field below the house would shew
A long deep pool with silent flow,
Just flow enough – no more! – to bring
The well-cocked fly inside the ring.

     And then, along my garden wall
I'd like this even best of all:
From bank to bank in hasty travel,
White water making music sweet,
White water rippling past my seat,
White water singing with the lark,
White water chuckling in the dark,
I want to hear it in my bed,
I want to hear it when I'm dead.

     So in the season, to and fro,
Along my fields will anglers go,
For every man who fishes fair
My brother is, and welcome there.
I'll see them pass with eager feet,
And greet them gaily from my seat.

     Sure well I know it's all a dream
     That has no substance, hope or gleam.
     And yet although I'm on the shelf,
     When I get talking to myself,
     I'm in a kingdom of my own
     Across the hills in dark Tyrone,
     And there I wave my stick with glee
     And swear that house belongs to me.

ALAS!

I caught a fish one dark September day.
The day the season ended: I was told,
It's no use fishing, for it's far too cold.
But still I fished: I flogged the estuary
For two long weary hours, and truth to say,
I never rose a thing. And then up rolled
A great trout's belly with its flash of gold,
I struck, and killed that fish in Conn's wee bay.

I slung it from my handkerchief and said,
'Now here's a fish will surely make some stir:
Five pounds on three X and a fly.' I fled
Homeward on wings. Fame was my splendid spur.
Alas for Fame! None saw me as I sped:
No, sir, I never met a soul. No, sir!

THE CENTENARIAN
Scotts Mills, Omagh

When I was young I was just a place
    With a wheen of wheels inside,
And a wooden wheel, a wooden wheel,
    A wheel that was my pride.
Black was the wheel on a grey stone wall,
    But where was a sweeter sound
Than its rumble up and its tumble down
    As it went splashing round?

    Hi for the hopper and the clinking wheels,
        And the dunder through the wall,
    And the running stones on the bedded stones,
        And the meal dust over all!
    Hi for the kiln and the good turf smell,
        And the corn so crisp and dry,
    For the fans that wail and the seeds that sail,
        And the shillen riding high!

They cut corn then with a ringing scythe,
    Or a sickle made to saw;
And a servant man would swing a flail
    While the farmer bottled straw.
The corn came here in a red farm cart,
    The white corn and the brown;
'Twas with candles dim or a lamp to trim
    I watched the dark come down.

The red farm cart is a tractor now,
    And the flails are long since fled,
And men must mow ere the binders go,
    But the scythes are rusted red.
On Omagh town the night comes down,
    Yet no man feels his way,
For my lamps are bright with a blinding light,
    And the darkness turns to day.

There are steeples three where there used to be
    A single steeple tall,
But the old-time kiln with the good turf smell
    Has vanished past recall:
And the drays that crept at a horse's walk,
    High-burdened from the mill,
Are lorries now no horse could haul,
    And they laugh at the Courthouse hill.

Green sallies shade the long mill lade
    Carnowen's streams supply;
With turbines low I face its flow
    And keep my old Stand-by:
But a current came no man could see
    With a power man learned to tame,
And it softly steals to my rolling wheels
    And my lamps that have no flame.

A hundred years is a hundred years,
    And a long way back in time,
But who dare say that I'm old and grey
    When I'm in my lusty prime?
And it's here alone, in dark Tyrone,
    My heart its homestead feels,
So I abide by the riverside
    Among my shining wheels.

But I think no shame of my wooden wheel,
    Or the past I have long outgrown,
For the wheel went round and the corn was ground,
    And so I served Tyrone:
And I made the meal, good oaten meal,
    From the day that I was born,
With the wooden wheel and the wheen of wheels
    And the stones that ground the corn.

BALLINTRAIN

Long, long ago I lived beside a river,
    And, now I'm old, I think I see it still,
And feel the breeze that makes the sallies shiver,
    And watch the sunlight flash on stream and rill.
And, howsoever far that I go roaming,
    I still think long till I am back again,
For then my heart, my pilgrim heart goes homing
    To that bright burn that flows in Ballintrain.

There's many a river I have found enchanting
    There's many a stream where I have joyed to be;
The tuneful Mourne with melody so haunting,
    The gracious Strule that is so fair to see;
Carnowen in its loveliness at Cranny,
    The wee Glenelly rushing after rain,
Yet still for me the loveliest of any
    Is that bright burn that flows in Ballintrain.

Above Remackin bridge I used to linger
    When trout-rings widened in the sunset cool;
Below Drumduff I searched with poking finger
    The old tin box before I fished the pool:
And still no riverside was more endearing,
    No road so happy as the sanded lane
That led me from the homestead of my rearing
    To yon bright burn that flows in Ballintrain.

My folk are gone, but God the kindly Giver
    Has made a place where I shall be with them,
And I shall see, one day, the shining river
    Whose streams make glad the New Jerusalem:
But still I hope that when the gates are swinging,
    The golden gates that shut out tears and pain,
Down past the Father's House I'll hear it singing,
    – A burn like that which flows in Ballintrain.

GOING BACK

I'm going soon across the sea
    Back home where I belong;
I'm tired of trees and jungle heat,
    And rivers with no song.
For I was born in old Tyrone,
    Where streams go singing down
The sweet and kindly hills of home
    That wear a heather crown.

    I'm going back to old Tyrone
        To seek a kinder sun,
    I'm going home no more to roam
        Till all my days are done.
    I've travelled far in peace and war.
        And found the travelling lone,
    But good old friends, when travel ends,
        I'll find in old Tyrone.

Here spreading trees shut out the breeze,
    They house no birds within;
I'd give them all for ash-trees tall,
    And scent of golden whin,
It's o'er the sea I want to be,
    Where winds are cool and fair,
And blackbirds sing in old Tyrone
    Among the bushes there.

Oh, there's a burn in old Tyrone
    That sings through Ballintrain;
Before I die, its lullaby
    I want to hear again.
And I'll not stay nor waste a day,
    Whatever may betide,
Until I hear that music clear
    In my own country-side.

HI! UNCLE SAM!

Hi! Uncle Sam!
>When freedom was denied you,
>And Imperial might defied you,
>Who was it stood beside you
>>At Quebec and Brandywine?
>And dared retreats and dangers,
>Red-coats and Hessian strangers,
>In the lean, long-rifled Rangers,
>>And the Pennsylvania Line?

Hi! Uncle Sam!
>Wherever there was fighting,
>Or wrong that needed righting,
>An Ulsterman was sighting
>>His Kentucky gun with care:
>All the road to Yorktown,
>From Lexington to Yorktown,
>From Valley Forge to Yorktown,
>>That Ulsterman was there!

Hi! Uncle Sam!
>Virginia sent her brave men,
>The North paraded grave men,
>That they might not be slave men,
>>But ponder this with calm:
>The first to face the Tory,
>And the first to lift Old Glory
>Made your war an Ulster story:
>>Think it over, Uncle Sam!

WHY?

The wind is dead,
    The water clear,
And overhead
    No clouds appear:
The sun is high,
    The river low,
Yet why must I
    A-fishing go?

On arches four
    The bridge is set,
But now no more
    Than two are wet.
The pool below
    Is strangely small
And weak in flow
    Along the wall.

The salmon redds
    Of winter-time
Are dry sand-beds
    Patchworked with slime:
And yonder where
    The Olives spin,
The stones are bare,
    The stream is thin.

Yet to be here
    In hawthorn shade,
My fishing gear
    Beside me laid,
Is not without
    Somewhat of gain,
Though sleepy trout
    My flies disdain.

A blackbird sings
　　Perched on a rail,
A wagtail swings
　　A lively tail.
A mallard's quack
　　Of warning gruff
Sends gliding back
　　Six balls of fluff.

Goldfinches ride
　　The thistle tops,
Out from its hide
　　A rabbit pops.
A gem in flight
　　Darts down the vale,
O heavenly sight!
　　Kingfisher! Hail!

Yes, to be here
　　Has much of gain,
Though skies are clear
　　And fishing vain:
For I meantime
　　Can be at ease
And make this rhyme
　　Myself to please.

My river brings
　　These joys to me,
So many things,
　　So much to see.
Wherefore as long
　　As rivers flow,
I'll sing their song,
　　And fishing go.

TULLYNEIL

On that green hill in dark Tyrone
    That lifts its shoulders broad
Above a house of weathered stone
    – A plain old house of God –
The whins embroider now the lea,
    The cattle come and go,
Crab-apple blossom, fair to see
    Warms up the whitethorn snow.

An oak-tree lifts his ancient head
    In majesty sedate,
The maple leaves are furnace red
    Down by the churchyard gate;
And that Te Deum, sweet and strong,
    That follows lifted rain
Is in a lofty blackbird's song
    Far answered up the lane.

Of old were often posted here
    Men swift to bare the steel,
In belted gown and fighting gear
    – The swordsmen of O'Neill.
But that was long and long ago
    Ere Hugh left land and home
To break his heart in exile slow
    And die in distant Rome.

The memory is misted now
    Of Con and Hugh and Shane,
For strangers came to speed the plough
    Across their great domain.
And yet, while Tullyneil is named
    Here in my countryside,
Something of what was feared and famed
    Abides, and will abide.

Enchantment waited here for me
    In boyhood's golden day,

And still each gate and hedge and tree
    Can sweep the years away,
And conjure pictures of the kind
    No canvas need retain,
For I can paint them in my mind
    And live my youth again.

There's splendour when the great seas roar
    Along a Northern strand
And break and pound the patient shore
    And fill the shining sand:
But I was born in old Tyrone
    And love the quiet things,
The burn that chuckles round a stone,
    The song a blackbird sings.

The little by-roads, free from dread,
    Where one has time to wait
And pat a horse that holds his head
    Across a roadside gate;
The summer hum of honey bees,
    Our Sabbath peace unflawed,
Our green God's acre in the trees,
    Our plain old house of God.

Such things are tethers to my feet
    When my departure nears;
These, and the old old friends I meet,
    Unmatched throughout the years,
Who learned with me in days long gone
    That two and two make four,
And toed with me a chalk line drawn
    Upon a schoolroom floor.

Here is their meeting-house, the place
    Where Sabbath prayer is made,
And here in Tullyneil's embrace
    Their dead and mine are laid.
So maybe on another day
    Lonesome I shall not feel
When I come back again to stay
    Content, in Tullyneil.

DRUMDUFF

The grass is green-springing on Drumduff hill,
The larks are loud-singing in Drumduff still;
But rot has long blackened the thatch that was gold,
And the hearth of my people is broken and cold.

Plum-blossom is falling snow white on the green,
The moor-fowl are calling, secure and unseen,
The bonnie brown heather still perfumes the air,
But the house on the hill-top is tumbled and bare.

No cheery cart-rattle enlivens the lane,
The byre has no cattle, the barn has no grain;
No man on his kailey comes here as of old,
The crickets are silent, the spiders are bold.

The nettles are nipping me now on the street
Where once there went tripping my mother's wee feet;
She was rocked in a cradle near yon broken wall,
Far away she sleeps deeper below a green pall.

The grass is green-springing on Drumduff hill,
The larks are loud-singing in Drumduff still;
Yet a sweetness so steadfast is far from enough
When the hearth of my people is cold in Drumduff.

FRAGMENT

As I grow old and sleep sometimes forsakes
The dragging hours from midnight to the dawn
I have my solace when remembrance wakes
To fetch me pictures of the years long gone:
Long gone indeed, for while my yesterdays
Are strangely dim and clouded in recall,
The far back things are vivid to my gaze
And joyous is my welcome to them all.

And strange it is that while my yesterdays
Are strangely dim and clouded in recall. . .